The Dignity of Difference

The Dignity of Difference

How to Avoid the Clash of Civilizations

JONATHAN SACKS

continuum
LONDON • NEW YORK

CONTINUUM
The Tower Building, 11 York Road, London, SE1 7NX
370 Lexington Avenue, New York, NY 10017–6503

www.continuumbooks.com

First published 2002

British Library Cataloguing in Publication Data
A catalogue record for this book is available from the British Library.

ISBN 0 8264 6397 5

Typeset by BookEns Ltd, Royston, Herts.
Printed and bound in Great Britain by MPG Books Ltd, Bodmin.

Contents

Acknowledgements

Behind every book is a story: in this case how a religious leader found himself caught up in conversations about the economics and politics of globalization. I owe a debt of gratitude to several individuals who convinced me that none of us can stand aside from critical reflection on what is happening to our world as a result of the hyperconnectedness and fragility of the global age. My thanks therefore go to Dr Klaus Schwab of the World Economic Forum, Jim Garrison of the State of the World Forum, and the organizers of the United Nations Millennium Peace Summit, each of whom invited me to share in their deliberations during the past two years, and to Professor John Dunning, who first persuaded me to write on these themes, and suggested a line of approach. I am also indebted to the Institute of Economic Affairs for asking me to deliver the 1998 Hayek Lecture, and to City University for the invitation to deliver the 2000 Mais Lecture, both of which set me thinking about trust, contract and covenant and the non-economic dimensions of economic systems.

Conversations with George Soros, Lord (Arnold) Weinstock and Noreena Hertz whetted my interest in globalization. Sir Stanley Kalms has constantly challenged me to address contemporary economic issues and is one of the most stimulating minds I know. Sir Sigmund Sternberg, a remarkable figure in both interfaith work and business ethics, has always encouraged my work in these two fields. I owe an especial debt to Chancellor of the Exchequer Gordon Brown for his consistent interest in the dialogue between faith, politics and economics, and for the strong commitment he has shown to the moral dimension of global economic policy.

One of the unexpected delights of becoming a religious leader has been the friendships I have made with leaders of other faiths, nationally and internationally, and these have convinced me that the world's great faiths have a significant potential role in conflict resolution and not merely, as many continue to believe, in conflict creation. One example of this – launched during the period I was writing this book – was the campaign Respect, which emerged out of a conversation between the Prince of Wales, the Archbishop of Canterbury and myself. The idea, supported by all faith groups in Britain, is that each religious and ethnic community should encourage its members to do an act of service or kindness to someone or some group of another faith or ethnicity – to extend a hand of help, in other words, *across* the boundaries of difference and thus turn communities outward instead of inward. Grassroots initiatives of this kind are vital in rebuilding trust in areas where it has broken down, and my warm appreciation goes to Tom Shebbeare and his colleagues at The Prince's Trust and the team at Timebank for turning this vision into a reality.

Most of my work would be impossible without my extraordinarily dedicated office team, and I thank them all, especially Syma Weinberg, Jeremy Newmark and Malcolm Lachs, for their support far beyond the call of duty. Joanna Benarroch and Sara King-Scott, with wondrous efficiency, helped me get the many books I needed for my research. I owe special thanks to Louise Greenberg, my indefatigable and ever-patient literary agent, and to Robin Baird-Smith, my publisher, who had faith in the project and sustained mine. As ever, it was my wife Elaine, son Joshua, daughter-in-law Eve, and daughters Dina and Gila, who put up with my absences and abstractions, listened to my ideas, and kept me going. I thank the Almighty for them and for the privilege of being alive at this hour, with all its conflicts and tensions. Rarely has He set humanity a tougher task than that of living in close proximity to difference – racial, ethnic, religious, cultural and economic – and the greater the task, the larger the challenge to our courage and moral imagination. I, for one, would not want it any other way.

Chapter 1

Prologue

When the Holy One created the first man, He took him and led him round all the trees of the Garden of Eden and said to him: 'Behold my works, how beautiful, how splendid they are. All that I have created, I created for you. Take care, therefore, that you do not destroy my world, for if you do, there will be no one left to repair what you have destroyed.'

(Midrash, *Ecclesiastes Rabbah*)

In January 2002 I stood at Ground Zero, site of the destruction of the World Trade Center on 11 September 2001. Standing beside me were representatives of the world's faiths, brought together by their participation in the World Economic Forum, which had moved from Davos, Switzerland, to New York as a gesture of solidarity to a city which had suffered so much trauma and loss. The Archbishop of Canterbury said a prayer. So did a Muslim imam. A Hindu guru from India recited a meditation and sprinkled rose petals on the site, together with holy water from the Ganges. The Chief Rabbi of Israel read a reflection he had written for the occasion. Another rabbi said kaddish, the traditional Jewish prayer for the dead. It was a rare moment of togetherness in the face of mankind's awesome powers of destruction. I found myself wondering at the contrast between the religious fervour of the hijackers and the no less intense longing for peace among the religious leaders who were there. The juxtaposition of good and evil, harmony and conflict, global peace and holy war, seemed to me a fitting metaphor for the century we have just begun. We have acquired fateful powers. We can heal or harm, mend or destroy on a scale unimaginable to previous generations. The stakes have never been higher, and the choice is ours.

This is a book about globalization, the challenges it raises, the good it brings, the suffering it causes, the resistances and resentments it generates. There have been many books written about the emerging global landscape, but all too few about the moral and spiritual issues involved.[1] Yet these are among the most important we must face if we are to enhance human dignity, improve the chances of peace and avoid Samuel Huntington's prediction of a clash of civilizations. Bad things happen when the pace of change exceeds our ability to change, and events move faster than our understanding. It is then that we feel the loss of control over our lives. Anxiety creates fear, fear leads to anger, anger breeds violence, and violence – when combined with weapons of mass destruction – becomes a deadly reality. The greatest single antidote to violence is *conversation*, speaking our fears, listening to the fears of others, and in that sharing of vulnerabilities discovering a genesis of hope. I have tried to bring a Jewish voice to what must surely become a global conversation, for we all have a stake in the future, and our futures have become inexorably intertwined.

This work, though, is not written for Jews alone, nor is it confined to conventionally religious themes. Too often in today's world, groups speak to themselves, not to one another: Jews to Jews, Christians to fellow Christians, Muslims to Muslims, business leaders, economists and global protesters to their respective constituencies. The proliferation of channels of communication – e-mail, chat-groups, the Internet, online journals, and the thousands of cable and satellite television channels – mean that we no longer broadcast. We narrowcast. Gone are the days where people of different views were forced to share an arena and thus meet and reason with their opponents. Today, we can target those who agree with us and screen out the voices of dissent. Those who wish to make their views known, do so by ways that catch the attention of the news – usually by some form of violence or protest, an event that can be captured by a dramatic image, a soundbite, and scenes of confrontation. Television news especially, with its short attention span, is no substitute for rational debate and serious engagement with contrary views. Conversation, the heartbeat of democratic politics, is dying and with it our chances of civic, let alone global, peace.

Had, for instance, our little group of faith leaders broken up in anger and disarray, it might have made the news. Meeting as it did in sombre and reflective harmony, it was hardly worthy of attention. One of the most important ideas of Harvard political philosopher John Rawls is that of 'public reason',[2] the process by which people in political debate use a language and logic accessible to all so that we can – in the prophet Isaiah's phrase – 'reason together'. The idea of reasoning together was dealt a fateful blow in the twentieth century by the collapse of moral language, the disappearance of 'I ought' and its replacement by 'I want', 'I choose', 'I feel'. Obligations can be debated. Wants, choices and feelings can only be satisfied or frustrated. Television, with its emphasis on the visual, creates a culture of sight rather than sound – the image that speaks louder than the word. Images evoke emotion. They do not, of themselves, generate understanding. The result is that the most visual protest, the angriest voice and the most extreme slogan win. If confrontation is news and conciliation not, we will have a culture of confrontation. That is destructive of the things on which our future will depend – our ability to understand and be understood by people whose cultures, creeds, values and interests conflict with ours and to whom, therefore, we must speak and listen. In setting out a Jewish perspective on matters that concern us all, I am making a commitment to public reason. When the visual image speaks louder than the still, small voice of reason and moderation, events like September 11 happen, and there will be more.

* * *

My argument will be twofold. Firstly, the economics and politics of globalization have an inescapable moral dimension. Their aim must be to enhance, not compromise, human dignity. Markets serve those who pay, but what of those who cannot pay? Politics is about the balance of power, but what of those who have no power? Economic systems create problems that cannot be resolved by economics alone. Politics raises questions that cannot be answered by political calculation alone. There is no escape from the wider issues of morality, and if we ignore them, history suggests that they will return in the form of anger, resentment and a burning sense of injustice, which will make our already fragile order more precarious still.

Secondly, great responsibility now lies with the world's religious communities. Against all expectation, they have emerged in the twenty-first century as key forces in a global age. Throughout Latin America, sub-Saharan Africa, the Philippines, Korea and China there has been a sweeping revival of evangelical Protestantism. An Islamic upsurge has affected every Muslim country from North Africa to South East Asia and Muslim communities elsewhere. The Catholic Church, numbering some 800 million people, was active in the fall of communism in east central Europe in 1989 (so alarmed at this were the Chinese that an official publication in 1992 warned, 'If China does not want such a scene to be repeated in its land, it must strangle the baby while it is still in the manger').[3] In conflict zones throughout the world – Northern Ireland, the Balkans, Chechnya, Tajikistan, the Middle East, Sudan, Sri Lanka, India, Kashmir, East Timor – they are at the cutting edge of confrontation, reminding us of Jonathan Swift's acid observation that we have 'just enough religion to make us hate one another but not enough to make us love one another'.

Religion can be a source of discord. It can also be a form of conflict resolution. We are familiar with the former; the second is far too little tried. Yet it is here, if anywhere, that hope must lie if we are to create a human solidarity strong enough to bear the strains that lie ahead. The great faiths must now become an active force for peace and for the justice and compassion on which peace ultimately depends. That will require great courage, and perhaps something more than courage: a candid admission that, more than at any time in the past, we need to search – each faith in its own way – for a way of living with, and acknowledging the integrity of, those who are not of our faith. Can we make space for difference? Can we hear the voice of God in a language, a sensibility, a culture not our own? Can we see the presence of God in the face of a stranger? Religion is no longer marginal to international politics. After a long period of eclipse, it has re-emerged with immense and sometimes destructive force. That is what lay behind an unusual assembly – and my first encounter with globalization – as the new millennium began.

* * *

On 28 August 2000, more than 2,000 religious leaders gathered in the United Nations building in New York. It was a dazzling sight. There were the saffron robes of the Tibetan monks, the grey vestments of Japanese shinto priests, Sufis in their distinctive hats, Sikhs in their turbans, the black robes of the imams, the blue and red sacred clothes of the reindeer people of north Sweden, Native Americans with their eagle bonnets, African priests in purple, Anglicans with their clerical collars and, it seemed, every other conceivable shade and shape of dress. Being there was like walking into a living lexicon of the religious heritage of mankind. Never before had there been such a gathering at the UN. In the great conference chamber normally reserved for politicians debating the issues of the day, here were men and women who devoted their lives not to the noise of now but to the music of eternity, not to the shifting sands of the international arena but to the inner landscape of the human spirit.

Yet despite the serene faces of the participants, the sense of urgency was palpable. The United Nations itself had designated 2001 as the International Year of Dialogue between Civilizations. The new world order following the end of the Cold War was rapidly turning into a new world disorder. The end of a single overarching confrontation between Soviet communism and the West had given rise not to peace but to a proliferating number of local conflicts between peoples who had previously lived together, if not in peace, then at least without bloodshed. Often, religion was a factor in the conflict – rarely as the cause, which was usually political or economic, but still as the fault line along which sides divided. This was what lay behind the gathering of religious leaders, a prelude to the assembly of 150 heads of state a week later. It was heralded as the Millennium World Peace Summit – an ambitious title for an ambitious undertaking.

The aim was to enlist leaders of every major faith community to the cause of global peace. Many of them had never been in such an assembly before. Used to preaching and teaching within their own communities, they found themselves suddenly caught up in a larger universe of many faiths and multiple languages. Given their profound differences, the degree of convergence was surprising. There were awkward moments, not least because there were so many voices needing to be heard. Yet there was a significant measure of consensus on the need for mutual respect and non-violent methods of conflict resolution, on shared responsibility for the future of the planet, our obligations to the poor and duties to protect the environment. At the end of four days of deliberations, mostly goodnatured and generous in tone, they signed a joint declaration of commitment to peace in its many dimensions.

One of the more moving moments came when an Eskimo from Greenland, Angaangaq Lyberth, quietly said to the audience, so remote from his normal world:

> About ten years ago now, one of my people came back to our village and reported a strange phenomenon. 'There is a trickle of water coming down the glacier. I think that the ice is melting.' Today that trickle has become a stream. So I say to you, while we sit here sharing words of peace: The ice is melting ... The ice is melting.

It summed up the mood of hope.

Barely more than a year later, on 11 September 2001, not far from the United Nations building where those words were said, two fully laden jumbo jets crashed into the World Trade Center and changed our world. The tragedy was freighted with symbolism. Two icons of global capitalism, the jet and the skyscraper, were turned into instruments of destruction. Office workers going about their daily routine found themselves suddenly implicated in a conflict whose epicentre was thousands of miles away and of whose very existence they may have been unaware. The terror itself was plotted by means of the Internet, encrypted e-mails and satellite phones. It was almost certainly planned with global television coverage in mind. The terrorists' methods were quintessentially modern, but their religious ideas were centuries old. Nothing could have demonstrated more vividly the vulnerability of our hyperconnected world and the unresolved tensions it contains. Suddenly, religion seemed less like a melting glacier than like a conflagration burning out of control. Far from being too much, too soon, our deliberations a year earlier seemed, if anything, too little, too late.

* * *

In the weeks and months that have passed, it has become ever more clear that we face great dangers in the coming century, and that we are not adequately prepared for them. On the one hand, globalization is bringing us closer together than ever before, interweaving our lives, nationally and internationally, in complex and inextricable ways. On the other, a new tribalism – a regression to older and more fractious loyalties – is driving us ever more angrily apart. One way or another, religion is and will continue to be, part of these processes. It can lead us in the direction of peace. But it can equally, and with high combustibility, lead us to war. Politicians have power, but religions have something stronger: they have influence. Politics moves the pieces on the chessboard. Religion changes lives. Peace can be agreed around the conference table; but unless it grows in ordinary hearts and minds, it does not last. It may not even begin.

Peace is a paradox. Many traditions praise it and decry conflict and war. Yet in war, even ordinary people become heroes. In pursuit of peace, even heroes are often afraid to take the risk. Those who show courage in the heat of battle are celebrated. Those who take risks for peace are all too often assassinated – among them Lincoln, Gandhi, Martin Luther King, Anwar El-

Sadat and Yitzhak Rabin. The pursuit of peace can come to seem to be a kind of betrayal. It involves compromise. It means settling for less than one would like. It has none of the purity and clarity of war, in which the issues – self-defence, national honour, patriotism, pride – are unambiguous and compelling. War speaks to our most fundamental sense of identity: there is an 'us' and a 'them' and no possibility of confusing the two. When, though, enemies shake hands, who is now the 'us' and who the 'them'? Peace involves a profound crisis of identity. The boundaries of self and other, friend and foe, must be redrawn. No wonder, then, that as Sir Henry Maine observed, 'War appears to be as old as mankind, but peace is a modern invention.'[4]

Something new, however, has entered the post-Cold War world. There were times when peace was imposed by empires. Between the mid-seventeenth and mid-twentieth centuries it became the province of nation-states under the doctrine of the balance of power. Following the Second World War it was sustained under the overarching confrontation of two superpowers and the Damocles' sword of nuclear destruction. Peace was never total, and in the twentieth century alone, more than 100 million people lost their lives in the course of war. Yet even then there were ground rules, conventions, arenas of diplomacy and calculations of risk, loss and cost. War was tragic, disastrous and devastating, but it was not wholly irrational.

September 11, however, heralds a new and frightening possibility, namely of non-state actors – individuals and small groups, hard to identify, harder still to locate, track down and bring to justice – capable of organizing globally and of wreaking havoc on a large scale in unpredictable ways. These are not groups driven by interests or *raisons d'état*. They, and those they enlist, are not bound by rational considerations. They are often driven by violent religious hatred. They are willing to commit, even righteously embrace, suicide as a means of entry into paradise. They make no distinctions between combatant and non-combatant, innocent or guilty, young or old, involved or disengaged. Within the foreseeable future they may have access to weapons of mass destruction. They have understood that the very interconnectedness of global societies – their openness and anonymity – constitute their vulnerability. This is not war in the conventional sense. In method it is something new. In motivation it is something very old indeed. It is conflict religionized, absolutized, and thus made immune to the accommodations and compromises of peace.

At such times, religious leaders have to take a stand. That is not to say we have the power to prevent extremism. Manifestly, we do not. The campaign against terror will not, in the first instance, be religious. It will be a complex operation involving intelligence-gathering, selective military action, the tracking of funds, weapons and lines of communication and sophisticated methods of screening and security. Yet religious believers cannot stand aside when people are murdered in the name of God or a sacred cause. When religion is invoked as a justification for conflict, religious voices must be raised in protest. We must withhold the robe of sanctity when it is sought as a cloak for violence and bloodshed. If faith is enlisted in the cause of war, there must be an equal and opposite counter-voice in the name of peace. *If religion is not part of a solution, it will certainly be part of the problem.*

A global age poses a difficult yet inescapable question to those who are loyal adherents of a religious tradition. Do we speak to and within the narrow loyalties of our faith, or does our faith itself give rise to a generosity of spirit capable of recognizing the integrity – yes, even the sanctity – of worlds outside our faith? No one should underestimate the difficulties of peace. There are times, as at the United Nations, when it seemed so simple. Every one of the religious leaders there could find words within his or her tradition that spoke of peace, in the world or within the soul, as a great and noble ideal. Yet even then an outsider could understand why religion is as often a cause of conflict as it is of conciliation. The peace spoken of was too often 'peace on our terms'. The argument was this: 'Our faith speaks of peace; our holy texts praise peace; therefore, if only the world shared our faith and our texts there would be peace.' Tragically, that path does not lead to peace. In this not-yet-fully-redeemed world, peace means living with those who have a different faith and other texts. There is a fundamental difference between the end-of-days peace of religious unity and the historical peace of compromise and coexistence. The pursuit of the former can sometimes be the most formidable enemy of the latter.

Throughout history until very recently, most people for most of their lives were surrounded by others with whom they shared a faith, a tradition, a way of life, a set of rituals and narratives of memory and hope. Under such circumstances it was possible to believe that our truth was the only truth; our way the only way. Outsiders were few; dissidents fewer still. That is not our situation today. We live in the conscious presence of difference. In the street, at work and on the television screen we constantly encounter cultures whose ideas and ideals are unlike ours. That can be experienced as a profound threat to identity. One of the great transformations from the twentieth to the twenty-first centuries is that whereas the former was dominated by the politics of *ideology*, we are now entering an age of the politics of *identity*. That is why religion has emerged, after a long eclipse, to become so powerful a presence on the world stage, because religion is one of the great answers to the question of identity. But that, too, is why we face danger. Identity divides. The very process of creating an 'Us' involves creating a 'Them' – the people not like us. In the very process of creating community within their borders, religions can create conflict across those borders.

Our situation at the beginning of the twenty-first century is like that of Europe at the beginning of the seventeenth century. Then as now, the landscape was littered with the debris of religious conflict, the result of the Reformation and the end of an era in which Europe was dominated by a single overarching power. It is fair to say that religion did not distinguish itself at that time. It was then that honest, thoughtful men and women began to say to themselves: if people of faith cannot live together in peace, despite their differences, then for the sake of the future we must find another way. The secularization of Europe, first in the sciences, then in the arts, then in politics and the structure of society, grew directly out of the failure of religion to meet the challenge of change. As one who deeply believes in the humanizing power of faith, and the stark urgency of coexistence at a time when weapons of mass destruction are accessible to extremist groups, I do not think we can afford to fail again. Time and again in recent years we have been reminded that religion is not what the European Enlightenment thought it would become: mute, marginal and mild. It is fire – and like fire, it warms but it also burns. And we are the guardians of the flame.

* * *

Two conversations are now necessary. One is between religious leaders on the one hand, and politicians and business leaders on the other, as to the direction globalization must take. Technology and the sheer pace and extent of global trade are transforming our world almost faster than we can bear. This has brought benefits to many, but distress, disruption and poverty to many others whose voice we must also hear. That, since the days of the Hebrew Bible, has been a classic task of faith and one of its most majestic virtues. Even Karl Marx, one of religion's greatest critics, noted that 'Religious suffering is at the same time an expression of real suffering and a protest against real suffering. Religion is the sigh of the oppressed creature, the feeling of a heartless world, the soul of soulless conditions.'[5] We must speak the silent cry of those who today suffer from want, hunger, disease, powerlessness and lack of freedom.

The liberal democracies of the West are ill-equipped to deal with such problems. That is not because they are heartless – they are not; they care – but because they have adopted mechanisms that marginalize moral considerations. Western politics have become more procedural and managerial. Not completely: Britain still has a National Health Service, and most Western countries have some form of welfare provision. But increasingly, governments are reluctant to enact a vision of the common good because – so libertarian thinkers argue – there is little substance we can give to the idea of the good we share. We differ too greatly. The best that can be done is to deliver the maximum possible freedom to individuals to make their own choices, and the means best suited to this is the unfettered market where we can buy whatever lifestyle suits us, this year, this month. Beyond the freedom to do what we like and can afford, contemporary politics and economics have little to say about the human condition. They give us inadequate guidance in knowing what to do in the face of the random brutalities of fate. We need to recover an older tradition – essentially a set of religious traditions – that spoke of human solidarity, of justice and compassion, and of the non-negotiable dignity of individual lives.

Globalization raises vast, even protean issues: too complex, perhaps, for any single mind or group to conceptualize, let alone confront in practice. What, then, can a religious perspective contribute? It cannot lie at the level of detail. The world's great faiths arose at the so-called 'axial age' of civilization, long before the rise of modernity. Yet there is much that a religious voice – more precisely, a range of religious voices – can add to the collective conversation on where we are, or should be, going. Faced with fateful choices, humanity needs wisdom, and religious traditions, alongside the great philosophies, are our richest resource of wisdom. They are sustained reflections on humanity's place in nature and what constitute the proper goals of society and an individual life. They build communities, shape lives and tell the stories that explain ourselves to ourselves. They frame the rituals that express our aspirations and identities. In uncharted territory one needs a compass, and the great faiths have been the compasses of mankind. In an age of uncertainty, they remind us that we are not alone, nor are we bereft of guidance from the past. The sheer tenacity of the great faiths – so much longer- lived than political systems and ideologies – suggests that they speak to something enduring in human character. Above all, it was religion that first taught human beings to look beyond the city-state, the tribe and the nation to humanity as a whole.[6] The world faiths are global phenomena whose reach is broader and in some respects deeper than the nation-state.

Judaism is one of those voices. The prophets of ancient Israel were the first to think globally, to conceive of a God transcending place and national boundaries and of humanity as a single moral

Insights from ancient prophets of Israel

community linked by a covenant of mutual responsibility (the covenant with Noah after the Flood). Equally, they were the first to conceive of society as a place where 'justice rolls down like water and righteousness like a never-ending stream' and of a future in which war had been abolished and peoples lived together in peace. Those insights and aspirations have lost none of their power.

No less significantly, Judaism was the first religion to wrestle with the reality of global dispersion. During the destruction of the First Temple in the sixth century BCE, Jews were transported to Babylon in the East or had escaped to Egypt in the West. By the time of the destruction of the Second Temple, in 70 CE, they had spread throughout much of Europe and Asia. For almost 2,000 years, scattered throughout the world, they continued to see themselves and be seen by others as a single people – the world's first global people. That experience forced Jews to reflect on many problems that are now the shared experience of mankind: how to maintain identity as a minority, how to cope with insecurity, and how to sustain human dignity in a world that seems often to deny it.[7] Judaism eventually gave rise to two other monotheisms, Christianity and Islam, that represent the faith of more than half of the six billion people alive today. There is much in common in the ethics of these three faiths, though each speaks in its own distinctive accent.

Reverence, restraint, humility, a sense of limits, the ability to listen and respond to human distress – these are not virtues produced by the market, yet they are attributes we will need if our global civilization is to survive and they are an essential part of the religious imagination. That is why I am heartened by the fact that in 2000 a dialogue took place between religious leaders and the World Bank; that since 2001 there has been a religious presence at the World Economic Forum; and that one of the most effective recent programmes of debt relief to developing economies – Jubilee 2000 – was a biblically based religious initiative, bringing together faith leaders and politicians. Religious leaders should never seek power, but neither may they abdicate their task of being a counter-voice in the conversation of mankind.

13

Globalization has led to a series of major public protests, in Seattle, Washington, Prague, London, Davos and wherever else business leaders and politicians have gathered to plan the economic future. These demonstrations have brought together a wide, lively and sometimes chaotic coalition of environmentalists, anti-capitalists and human rights activists, bound together in their sense – which I share – that something is going wrong. In Chapter 2 I summarize the most significant effects of globalization, some positive, others deeply disturbing. In the central chapters of this book I try to disentangle these complex processes into six dimensions.

The first is the way global phenomena undermine our sense of moral responsibility. In the past it was relatively easy to identify who was doing what to whom. It is no longer. The global market moves in response to billions of transactions. Electronic media offer an almost open-ended multiplicity of channels of communication. Nation-states have ever less power to shape developments in the economy, the political arena and the environment, all of which spill over national borders. Corporations have become increasingly shadowy entities, outsourcing many of their operations and able to move funds and functions at a moment's notice. Who, then, is the author of events? Is the world now out of control? Can we use ethical language any more when the link between individual agents, actions and consequences has become so tenuous? In Chapter 4 I argue that we can and must if we are not to abdicate responsibility for the future.

The second is the market economy itself. Many of the global protestors oppose the free market in principle. I argue in Chapter 5 that this opposition is mistaken, though its concerns are justified. The free market is the best means we have yet discovered for alleviating poverty and creating a human environment of independence, dignity and creativity. Most importantly, the market embodies an idea that is central to the argument of the book as a whole, namely that *difference* is the source of value, and indeed of society itself. It is precisely because we are not the same as individuals, nations or civilizations that our exchanges are non-zero-sum encounters. Because each of us has something someone else lacks, and we each lack something someone else has, we gain by interaction. That is what makes trade the most compelling counterforce to war.

The market, however, generates unequal outcomes and the faster it moves the more glaring the inequalities to which it gives rise. Within and between nations, these have now become unacceptably large. The concentration of the world's wealth into relatively few hands while millions of children live in poverty, ignorance and disease is a scandal which is no longer sustainable. One does not have to be a confirmed egalitarian to believe that such extremes are a scar on the face of humanity. How, though, are we to think through the responsibilities of the rich to the poor? What are the criteria of distributive justice? In Chapter 6 I suggest that the biblical concept of *tzedakah*, with its basic idea of the economic requirements of human dignity is more helpful than the Western polarity of charity and justice.

One of the drivers of globalization is the revolution in information technology. Does this have an ethical dimension? In Chapter 7 I tell the story of the three previous revolutions – the birth of writing, the alphabet and printing – to show how each created new social and political possibilities. A religious perspective is particularly helpful here because, in ways that are not well known, each revolution gave rise to new forms of civilization: writing to 'cosmological' societies, the alphabet to monotheism, and printing to the Reformation. What the effects of the fourth revolution, instantaneous global communication, will be, we cannot know, but we can already say what it requires from us, namely the primacy of education among the priorities of international aid. Information technologies democratize access to knowledge, and one of our aims must be to bring every child on earth within its radius. Education is the single greatest key to human dignity.

Danger arises in any social transformation when one institution exceeds its proper bounds and colonizes areas that have a different logic and dynamic. There were times – the Middle Ages – when this was true of religion. In the eighteenth century it became true of science. In the nineteenth and twentieth centuries it was true of politics. In the twenty-first century it has become true of the market. Monetary exchange is the appropriate mechanism for some transactions but not all. Society depends on the existence of certain relationships that stand outside economic calculation: among them, families, communities, congregations and voluntary associations. These are the institutions of civil society, and they have become seriously eroded in consumption-driven cultures. In Chapter 8, I show how developments in games theory and sociobiology have shown that the survival of any group depends not only on competition but also on habits of co-operation, and that these are endangered by the intrusion of the logic of the marketplace into relationships that I call 'covenantal' as opposed to contractual.

The danger posed by the global economy to the natural environment is well known. We are damaging the biosphere in ways that will be deeply harmful to future generations. How, though, do we conceptualize our duties to nature and to generations not yet born? Post-Enlightenment ethics finds it difficult to construct bonds of moral obligation here. Neither nature nor persons not yet in existence are moral subjects. How then can we have duties to them? In Chapter 9 I suggest that we are best guided by a more ancient wisdom: that we do not, severally or collectively, own nature but instead hold it in trust on behalf of those who will come after us. We are guests and guardians on earth.

There is an immense temptation, in the face of challenges as complicated as the multiple developments known as globalization, either to abdicate responsibility to experts, or to the course of history itself, or else to simplify by opposing the market and all its works. These cures are worse than the disease. The market is a mechanism, no more, no less, and what matters are the constraints we place on it and the direction in which we seek to go. That requires serious, engaged conversation between us – all of us, for we are all affected by these developments – and the politicians, economists and business leaders whose decisions affect the global economy. Single-issue campaigns and global protests are important but not enough, because the unfolding world order is not a single issue, and because protest is only a prelude to, not a substitute for, nuanced argument and the building of consensus between conflicting interests.

My own view, and it has shaped my presentation here, is that under conditions of maximal uncertainty, we are best guided by relatively simple moral principles – I call them control, contribution, creativity, co-operation, compassion and conservation, and suggest that these six Cs are the prelude to a seventh – a new global covenant of human solidarity. These are not meant as decision procedures but as compass bearings, allowing us to judge whether we are moving in the right direction or not. What is essential, though, is the concept of a direction. My own view – it is a religious one, but one does not have to be religious to share it – is that economic systems are to be judged by their impact on human dignity. An order that systematically deprives a significant proportion of mankind of fundamental dignities is indefensible. That does not mean abandoning the global market, but it does mean taking seriously a set of non-market values which must be factored in to our decisions about the future.

* * *

There is, though, a second conversation, no less urgent and important, to be had between religions, or what Huntington calls 'civilizations'. Can we live together? Can we make space for one another? Can we overcome long histories of estrangement and bitterness? Here I have not hesitated to be radical, and I have deliberately chosen to express that radicalism in religious terms. I believe that globalization is summoning the world's great faiths to a supreme challenge, one that we have been able to avoid in the past but can do so no longer. Can we find, in the human other, a trace of the Divine Other? Can we recognize God's image in one who is not in my image? There are times when God meets us in the face of a stranger. The global age has turned our world into a society of strangers. That is not a threat to faith but a call to a faith larger and more demanding than we had sometimes supposed it to be. Can I, a Jew, hear the echoes of God's voice in that of a Hindu or Sikh or Christian or Muslim or in the words of an Eskimo from Greenland speaking about a melting glacier? Can I do so and feel not diminished but enlarged? What then becomes of my faith, which until then had encompassed the world and must now make space for another faith, another way of interpreting the world?

Here I must make an autobiographical admission. I am not a liberal Jew. My faith is orthodox. I am used to being called, by my liberal colleagues, a fundamentalist, and it is precisely here that contemporary challenge is most acute. The revivals in most of the world's faiths in recent decades have been at the conservative rather than liberal end of the spectrum. The power of conservative religious movements has been precisely the fact that they represent protests against, rather than accommodations to, late modernity. They are expressions of a deep dismay at some of the side-effects of global capitalism: its inequities, its consumerism and exploitation, its failure to address widespread poverty and disease, its juggernaut insensitivity to local traditions and cultures, and the spiritual poverty that can go hand in hand with material wealth. It is religion not so much in its modern but in its countermodern guise that has won adherents in today's world, and it is here that the struggle for tolerance, coexistence and non-violence must be fought.

The late Sir Isaiah Berlin, a man I knew and respected, summed up the liberal creed in a quotation he made famous at the end of his great essay, *Two Concepts of Liberty*: 'to realise the relative validity of one's convictions, and yet stand for them unflinchingly, is what distinguishes a civilised man from a barbarian'.[8] That is a noble sentiment. To it, however, one of liberalism's most eloquent critics, Michael Sandel, replied: 'If one's convictions are only relatively valid, why stand for them unflinchingly?'[9] That has become a reverberating question. If freedoms of speech and association are mere conventions of Western modernity, by what right do I criticize those who reject them as a form of decadence? If respect for human life is only one value among many, what grounds have I for opposing the suicide bomber who believes that by murdering others he is securing his place in paradise?

Relativism is too weak to resist the storm winds of religious fervour. Only an equal and opposite fervour can do that. I do not believe that the sanctity of human life and the inalienable freedoms of a just society are relative. They are religious absolutes. They flow directly from the proposition that it was not we who created God in our image but God who made us in His. They belong to the very tradition that Jews, Christians and Muslims – who have spent so much of their history in mutual hostility – share. Healing must come from the religious experiences of those whose lives are governed by those experiences. It must come, if anywhere, from the heart of the whirlwind itself.

This means that each of us who belong to a faith must wrestle with the sources of extremism within our own faith. Judaism, Christianity and Islam are religions of revelation – faiths in which God speaks and we attempt to listen. One of the paradoxes of Judaism is that, though it is a religion of commands (*mitzvot*), biblical Hebrew contains no word that means 'to obey'. Instead it uses the word *shema*, which means to hear, to understand and to respond – to *listen* in the fullest range of senses. I believe that God is summoning us to a new act of listening, going back to the sources of our faith and hearing in them something we missed before, because we did not face these challenges, this configuration of dilemmas before. In religions of revelation, discoveries are re-discoveries, a discernment of something that was always there but not necessarily audible from where our ancestors stood. God's word is for all time, but our act of listening is of *this* time; and the challenge is to discern within that word, as it speaks to us now, a narrative of hope.

In Chapter 3 I propose a revolutionary argument: that a certain paradigm that has dominated Western thought, religious *and* secular, since the days of Plato is mistaken and deeply dangerous. It is the idea that, as we search for truth or ultimate reality we progress from the particular to the universal. Particularities are imperfections, the source of error, parochialism and prejudice. Truth, by contrast, is abstract, timeless, universal, the same everywhere for everyone. Particularities breed war; truth begets peace, for when everyone understands the truth, conflict

19

dissolves. How could it be otherwise? Is not tribalism but another name for particularity? And has not tribalism been the source of conflict through the ages?

There is something seductive about this idea and it has held many minds captive. Alfred North Whitehead once said that Western philosophy was 'a series of footnotes to Plato'. He might have put it more strongly: Not just philosophy but Western religion has been haunted by Plato's ghost. The result is inevitable and tragic. If all truth – religious as well as scientific – is the same for everyone at all times, then if I am right, you are wrong. If I care about truth I must convert you to my point of view, and if you refuse to be converted, beware. From this flowed some of the great crimes of history and much human blood.

Western civilization has known five universalist cultures: ancient Greece, ancient Rome, medieval Christianity and Islam, and the Enlightenment. Three were secular, two religious. They brought inestimable gifts to the world, but they also brought great suffering, most notably though not exclusively to Jews. Like a tidal wave they swept away local customs, ancient traditions and different ways of doing things. They were to cultural diversity what industrialization is to biodiversity. They extinguished weaker forms of life. They diminished difference.

Today we are living through the sixth universal order: global capitalism. It is the first to be driven not by a set of ideas but by a series of institutions, among them the market, the media, multinational corporations and the Internet. But its effect is no less profound. It threatens all things local, traditional and particular. September 11 happened when two universalist cultures, global capitalism and an extremist form of Islam, each profoundly threatening to the other, met and clashed.

It is time we exorcized Plato's ghost, clearly and unequivocally. Universalism must be balanced with a new respect for the local, the particular, the unique. There are indeed moral universals – the Hebrew Bible calls them 'the covenant with Noah' and they form the basis of modern codes of human rights. But they exist to create space for cultural and religious difference: the sanctity of human life, the dignity of the human person, and the freedom we need to

20

be true to ourselves while being a blessing to others. I will argue that the proposition at the heart of monotheism is not what it has traditionally been taken to be: one God, therefore one faith, one truth, one way. To the contrary, it is that *unity creates diversity*. The glory of the created world is its astonishing multiplicity: the thousands of different languages spoken by mankind, the hundreds of faiths, the proliferation of cultures, the sheer variety of the imaginative expressions of the human spirit, in most of which, if we listen carefully, we will hear the voice of God telling us something we need to know. That is what I mean by *the dignity of difference*.

This is a large and difficult idea, and I arrived at it only after much wrestling with the place of religion in the modern and postmodern world. I have spent much time in conversation with leaders of other faiths. I have cherished my friendships with Christian leaders and many others – Hindu, Sikh, Buddhist, Jain, Zoroastrian and Bahai. No less significantly, I have found an instant rapport with the representatives of Islam, not only from Britain but also those from the Middle East. In Britain and the international arena we have worked together, developing relationships that have allowed us – especially in the tense times that have come in the wake of September 11 – to dampen anger, fight the flames of local hostilities, and generate, through our shared fears, a sense of solidarity and goodwill.

But I have also been conscious of something left unsaid. Often, when religious leaders meet and talk, the emphasis is on similarities and commonalities, as if the differences between faiths were superficial and trivial. That is not, however, what comes to the fore at times of conflict. It is then that what seem to an outsider to be minor variations take on immense significance, dividing neighbourhoods and turning erstwhile friends into enemies. Freud called this 'the narcissism of small differences'. There is nothing so slight that it cannot, under pressure, be turned into a marker of identity and thus of mutual estrangement. We need, in other words, not only a theology of commonality – of the universals of mankind – but also a theology of difference: why it exists, why it matters, why it is constitutive of our humanity, why it represents the will of God.

21

The dignity of difference is more than a religious idea. It is the overarching theme that links the various strands of the argument I have constructed in the chapters that follow. To a remarkable degree, modernity was meant to be the triumphal march of a single cluster of interrelated ideas. Its model was science, its discourse, reason shorn of the accretions of tradition. Via market exchange and the division of labour it would generate wealth. Through industrialization and technology it would conquer nature. By utilitarian calculation it would maximize happiness. The world would become one giant satisfaction-producing machine delivering ever-larger yields of that measure-of-all-things called 'progress'. That myth, noble but radically inadequate to the human situation, still survives among market fundamentalists and fellow believers who maintain that maximal deregulation in all spheres of human activity will, of itself, achieve what Leibniz once believed was the province of God, namely, all for the best in the best of all possible worlds.

I have suggested a different model and metaphor. The world is not a single machine. It is a complex, interactive ecology in which diversity – biological, personal, cultural and religious – is of the essence. Any proposed reduction of that diversity through the many forms of fundamentalism that exist today – market, scientific or religious – would result in a diminution of the rich texture of our shared life, a potentially disastrous narrowing of the horizons of possibility. Nature, and humanly constructed societies, economies and polities, are systems of ordered complexity. That is what makes them creative and unpredictable. Any attempt to impose on them an artificial uniformity in the name of a single culture or faith, represents a tragic misunderstanding of what it takes for a system to flourish. Because we are different, we each have something unique to contribute, and every contribution counts. A primordial instinct going back to humanity's tribal past makes us see difference as a threat. That instinct is massively dysfunctional in an age in which our several destinies are interlinked. Oddly enough, it is the market – the least overtly spiritual of contexts – that delivers a profoundly spiritual message: that it is through exchange that difference becomes a blessing, not a curse. When difference leads to war, both sides lose. When it leads to mutual enrichment, both sides gain.

Crises happen when we attempt to meet the challenges of today with the concepts of yesterday. That is why nothing less than a paradigm shift may be needed to prevent a global age becoming the scene of intermittent but destructive wars. I speak from within the Jewish tradition, but I believe that each of us within our own traditions, religious or secular, must learn to listen and be prepared to be surprised by others. We must make ourselves open to their stories, which may profoundly conflict with ours. We must even, at times, be ready to hear of their pain, humiliation and resentment and discover that their image of us is anything but our image of ourselves. We must learn the art of conversation, from which truth emerges not, as in Socratic dialogues, by the refutation of falsehood but from the quite different process of letting our world be enlarged by the presence of others who think, act, and interpret reality in ways radically different from our own. We must attend to the particular, not just the universal. For when universal civilizations clash, the world shakes, and lives are lost. We will make peace only when we learn that God loves difference and so, at last, must we. God has created many cultures, civilizations and faiths but only one world in which to live together – and it is getting smaller all the time.

NOTES

1. Among the books that consider the moral dimension are Booth et al. 2001; Bentley and Jones 2001; and Stackhouse 2000 and 2001.
2. Rawls 1993, pp. 212–54; 1999, pp. 129–80.
3. Samuel Huntington, 'Religious Persecution and Religious Relevance in Today's World', in Abrams 2001, pp. 60–61.
4. See Howard 2000.
5. See Cupitt 1984, pp. 139–47.
6. Fukuyama 1999, pp. 231–45.
7. See Sacks 2001.
8. Berlin 2002, p. 217.
9. Sandel 1984, p. 8.

Chapter 2

Globalization and its Discontents

Globalization divides as much as it unites; it divides as it unites – the causes of division being identical with those which promote the uniformity of the globe.

(Zygmunt Bauman, *Globalization*)

The year: 2020. Dawn breaks on a world of global prosperity and peace. Information technology and high-speed communication have doubled real incomes in the space of 20 years. The spread of birth control techniques has finally removed the danger of overpopulation. Genetically modified crops and disease-resistant strains have increased food production to the point where starvation is a thing of the past. Using the latest curricula, downloaded by Internet, schools in African villages have reached the level of their Western counterparts. International agreements on employment, pay and work conditions have put an end to the sweatshops, child labour and low pay that, at the beginning of the twenty-first century, were the source of so much inequity and exploitation. Low-cost medical treatments have brought AIDS, TB and many other forms of disease under control. Genetic intervention has opened the way to preventing hereditary illness and disability. Research on the human genome has enabled doctors to alter the genetic switches responsible for aging. Life expectancy of 120 years is no longer a rarity. Observers agree that humanity is in the midst of a new golden age.

The time: 2020. The world has just been rocked by the latest terrorist attack on New York. A so-called 'dirty bomb' has spread nuclear waste over a wide area centred on Manhattan. As many as 20 million people may be affected. Meanwhile, in a co-ordinated attack on the subway systems of London, Paris, Munich and Rome, canisters containing deadly chemicals have been released in crowded stations. The toll of casualties is expected to be in the thousands. Air travel is at a standstill, following a series of highly publicized hijackings. Government collapses in Africa have left that continent reeling from an outbreak of vicious local wars. Meanwhile, revolutions in Egypt, Jordan, Algeria and Saudi Arabia have created a Middle East dominated by fundamentalist regimes. The global economy is in a state of collapse and, in one country after another, unemployment is at a record high. Throughout the West, city centres and public spaces have become derelict and decaying no-go zones with vagabond populations of drug addicts, the homeless and the violent. The wealthy live in gated enclaves protected by massive, privately funded security systems. Hundreds of thousands die annually as a result of freak weather conditions – droughts, floods and typhoons – brought about by global warming. Pollution has made it impossible to walk in city streets without a protective mask. Most commentators agree that the world is in the midst of a new dark age.

Two scenarios, equally possible, and between them defining what is at stake in the years ahead. Uncertainty is constitutive of the human situation: whatever else we know, we can never know what tomorrow will bring. Yet there are degrees of uncertainty, and the sheer pace of change in the twenty-first century in almost every aspect of life – economic, political, cultural and techno-logical – is sweeping away many of the continuities that allowed previous generations to look forward to the future with confidence.

Already in the early twentieth century Alfred North Whitehead noted a qualitative change in our experience of time. In the past, he said, 'the time-span of important change was considerably longer than that of a single human life'. Most people inhabited a world whose contours were recognizably the same when they were old as when they were young. 'Today the time-span is considerably shorter than that of a human life', and it has continued to accelerate.[1] To give just one example: I have on my shelves a book of futurology, published in 1990, entitled *Megatrends 2000*. One word is conspicuous by its absence: the word 'Internet'.[2] In a post-presidential address, Bill Clinton noted that when he took up office in 1993 there were a mere 50 registered websites. By the time he left office in 2000 there were upwards of 350 million.[3] Change has become part of the texture of life itself, and there are few things harder to bear than constant flux and uncertainty.

Globalization – the interconnectedness of the world through new systems of communication – is one of the great transformations in history, comparable to the shift from the hunter-gatherer age to the era of agriculture, or from feudalism to industrialism. Like every other major transition, it gives rise to deep anxieties, evident in our time in the protests of environmentalists, human rights activists and anti-capitalists who have gathered in Seattle, Washington, Prague, Quebec City and Genoa, and wherever else there has been a gathering of business leaders and politicians to chart the world economic future. It is hard not to sympathize with the protesters. We seem caught, in Matthew Arnold's words, 'between two worlds, one dead, the other powerless to be born'. What is specific to our present situation is the sense that change is running ahead of our ability to chart a course for a shared future. Our technological powers grow daily, while our moral convictions become ever more hesitant and confused. What is it about globalization that makes us feel as if we were on a journey without a map, in a car that is out of control?

* * *

The concept of globalization is not new. Almost 400 years ago, John Donne gave it one of its most memorable expressions:

All mankinde is of one Author, and is one volume ... No
man is an Iland, intire of it selfe; every man is a peece of the
Continent, a part of the maine; if a Clod bee washed away
by the Sea, Europe is the less, as well as if a Promontorie
were, as well as if a Mannor of thy friends or of thine owne
were; any mans death diminishes me; because I am involved
in Mankinde; And therefore never send to know for whom
the bell tolls; It tolls for thee.[4]

International commerce,[5] practised extensively by the Phoenicians, goes back almost to the dawn of civilization. The great
maritime adventures, beginning in the fifteenth century, of Zheng
He, Vasco de Gama, Magellan and Columbus created new trade
routes and a growth of long-distance exchange. Further
momentum was added by the development of accurate navigation
instruments, the growth of banks and the funding of risk, and the
birth of giant international businesses such as the Dutch East
India Company. Industrialization, the spread of railways and the
invention of the telegraph added impetus in the course of the
nineteenth century. The integration of distant regions into a single
international economy has been a continuous process, extending
back for many centuries. A restless spirit has led mankind to travel
ever further in search of the new, the remote and the
undiscovered. Opening the Great Exhibition in London in
1851, Prince Albert made a speech that could be repeated almost
verbatim a century and a half later:

[W]e are living at a period of most wonderful transition
which tends rapidly to accomplish that great end to which
indeed all history points – the realization of the unity of
mankind ... The distances which separated the different
nations and parts of the globe are rapidly vanishing before
the achievements of modern invention, and we can traverse
them with incredible ease ... [T]hought is communicated
with the rapidity, and even by the power, of lightning ...
The products of all quarters of the globe are placed at our
disposal, and we have only to choose which is the best and

cheapest for our purposes, and the powers of production are entrusted to the stimulus of competition and capitalism.[6]

In one sense, then, the world we inhabit is a logical outcome of the legacy of our ancestors, the latest stage in a journey begun millennia ago.[7] But there are changes in degree which become changes in kind. The speed and scope of advances in modern communications technology have altered conditions of existence for many, perhaps most, of the world's six billion inhabitants. The power of instantaneous global communication, the sheer volume of international monetary movements, the internationalization of processes and products and the ease with which jobs can be switched from country to country have meant that our interconnectedness has become more immediate, vivid and consequential than ever before. It is one thing for a poet such as Donne to conjure a metaphysical idea, quite another to experience it daily.

Global capitalism is a system of immense power, from which it has become increasingly difficult for nations to dissociate themselves. More effectively than armies, it has won a battle against rival systems and ideologies, among them fascism, communism and socialism, and has emerged as the dominant option in the twenty-first century for countries seeking economic growth. Quite simply, it delivered what its alternatives merely promised: higher living standards and greater freedoms. Countries that have embraced the new economy – among them Singapore, South Korea, Taiwan, Thailand, China, Chile, the Dominican Republic, India, Mauritius, Poland and Turkey – have seen spectacular rises in living standards.[8] Improvements in agriculture have meant that while, prior to industrialization, it took the majority of a country's workforce to produce the food it needed, today in advanced economies the figure is around 2 per cent.[9] Throughout the developed world, advances in medicine and healthcare have reduced infant mortality and raised life expectancy. The average supermarket in the West sets before consumers a range of choices that, a century ago, would have been beyond the reach of kings.

But globalization has immensely differential and destabilizing effects. Its benefits are not spread evenly. There are winners and losers, within and between countries. The 'digital divide' has heightened inequalities. The average North American consumes five times more than a Mexican, ten times more than a Chinese, 30 times more than an Indian. There are 1.3 billion people – 22 per cent of the world's population – living below the poverty line; 841 million are malnourished; 880 million are without access to medical care. One billion lack adequate shelter; 1.3 billion have no access to safe drinking water; 2.6 billion go without sanitation.[10] Among the children of the world, 113 million – two-thirds of them girls – go without schooling; 150 million are malnourished; 30,000 die each day from preventable diseases.[11]

In eighteen countries, all African, life expectancy is less than 50 years. In Sierra Leone it is a mere 37 years. Infant mortality rates are higher than one in ten in 35 countries, mostly in Africa but including Bangladesh, Bolivia, Haiti, Laos, Nepal, Pakistan and Yemen.[12] More than 80 countries have seen per capita incomes drop in the past ten years. By the end of the millennium, the top fifth of the world's population had 86 per cent of the world's GDP while the bottom fifth had just 1 per cent. The assets of the world's three richest billionaires were more than the combined wealth of the 600 million inhabitants of the least-developed countries.[13] The enormous wealth of the few contrasts starkly with the misery of the many and jars our sense of equity and justice.

Within the developed countries themselves, the gains have been highly selective. In the United States in the past 20 years 97 per cent of the increase in income has gone to the top 20 per cent of families, while the bottom fifth have seen a 44 per cent reduction in earnings. By 1996 Britain had the highest proportion in Europe of children living in poverty, with 300,000 of them worse off in absolute terms than they had been 20 years before.[14] Jobs have become less secure. There has been a move from lifelong careers to part-time, temporary and provisional employment. Meanwhile, under the pressure of open markets, financial deregulation and international competition, the welfare services and safety-nets that in the post-war years protected people in

Britain and America from the effects of unemployment have been reduced. The economic climate has become harsher and social solidarity more frayed.

The entire social environment worldwide has become less predictable, more prone to sudden and drastic change. The ability to shift production from place to place in response to currency fluctuations and wage rates means that jobs – not only in manufacturing industries but also in management and services – have become vulnerable. The massive flows of international finance that enter a new economy, fuelling speculative investment and property booms, can just as rapidly exit, leaving in their wake bankruptcies and vast swathes of unemployment. Whole economies are destabilized. Indebted nations, turning for help to international financial institutions, can find themselves subject to imposed economic disciplines that may have much to do with the protection of investors but little to do with the provision of long-term infrastructure and sustainable growth for their own populations.

Inequality within and between countries has existed before. What is new in our situation is our consciousness of it. The philosopher David Hume noted that our sense of empathy diminishes as we move outward from the members of our family to our neighbours, our society and the world. Traditionally, our sense of involvement with the fate of others has been in inverse proportion to the distance separating us and them. What has changed is that television and the Internet have effectively abolished distance. They have brought images of suffering in far-off lands into our immediate experience. Our sense of compassion for the victims of poverty, war and famine, runs ahead of our capacity to act. Our moral sense is simultaneously activated and frustrated. We feel that something should be done, but what and how and by whom?

Nor has globalization been only economic. It has been cultural as well. The Internet, cable and satellite television and the global presence of megacorporations have brought about a huge internationalization of images and artefacts – what Benjamin Barber calls McWorld.[15] The same jeans, T-shirts, trainers, soft drinks, fast-food stores, music and films can be seen on the streets of almost every major city on earth, and in many remote villages also. The world they represent is overwhelmingly American, and it tends to overwhelm local traditions, which are preserved, if at all, as tourist attractions. This too is deeply threatening to the integrity and dignity of non-Western civilizations. It is often difficult for the West to understand how alien, even decadent, its culture appears to those who experience it as a foreign importation. The emphasis on consumption is seen as trivializing to those with ancient spiritual heritages, and deeply exclusionary to those who are the losers in the race to riches.

* * *

Even before the anti-globalization movement was under way, concerns had already been expressed in the West about the impact of a market-led consumer culture on social institutions. As early as 1947 Joseph Schumpeter had warned that 'Capitalism creates a critical frame of mind which, after having destroyed the moral authority of so many other institutions, in the end turns against its own.'[16] Throughout the liberal democracies of the West, families and communities have been in decline, leading to new concentrations of poverty and social breakdown. Within a generation, especially among children, there has been a three- to ten-fold increase in stress-related syndromes, from psychiatric illness to eating disorders, drug and alcohol abuse, violence, crime, suicides and suicide attempts.[17] Individuals find themselves bereft of the support from family members, friends and neighbours whose presence was often a lifeline in earlier times.

Neighbourhoods in many Western cities have become ever more economically segregated. Because of the rise in crime, those with the means to do so have moved to gated communities and 'gilded ghettos'. Public spaces have grown fewer, their place taken by shopping malls and entertainment complexes, open only to those with the ability to pay. There is less mixing than there once was between different economic classes and age groups, and with it a breakdown of that hard-to-define element of social solidarity known as 'trust'. The well-to-do are less likely to use public services and have thus ceased to be campaigners for their improvement. Robert Reich's description was telling: he called it 'the secession of the successful'.[18]

Not only has the dominance of the market had a corrosive effect on the social landscape. It has also eroded our moral vocabulary, arguably our most important resource in thinking about the future. In one of the most influential books of recent times, *After Virtue*, Alasdair MacIntyre argued that 'We possess indeed simulacra of morality, we continue to use many of the key expressions. But we have – very largely, if not entirely – lost our comprehension, both theoretical and practical, of morality.'[19] The very concept of ethics (Bernard Williams called it 'that peculiar institution')[20] has become incoherent. Increasingly, we have moved to talking about efficiency (how to get what you want) and therapy (how not to feel bad about what you want). What is common to both is that they have more to do with the mentality of marketing (the stimulation and satisfaction of desire) than of morality (what *ought* we to desire). In the public domain, the two terms that dominate contemporary discourse are *autonomy* and *rights*, which share the mentality of the market by emphasizing choice while ruling out the possibility that there might be objective grounds for making one choice rather than another. This has made it very difficult for us to deliberate collectively about some of the most fateful choices, environmental, political and economic, humanity has ever faced. It is difficult to talk about the common good when we lose the ability to speak about duty, obligation and restraint, and find ourselves only with desires clamouring for satisfaction.

Even if our moral imagination were in good order, many of the issues posed by globalization would tax the resources of conventional ethics. This was the case argued, in the 1980s, by one of the prophets of the technological age, Hans Jonas. In his *The Imperative of Responsibility*, he argued that modernity was redefining the parameters of human action and choice.[21] Traditional ethics saw action in terms of its immediate effect on others who were usually close to hand. Nowadays we are aware of the long-term effects of human behaviour on those who are distant from us, whether in space or time (generations not yet born). We also face the problem of thinking about actions, insignificant in themselves, which none the less have a cumulative impact, such as the effect of aerosols or fuel emissions on the earth's atmosphere.

Previous generations could take the natural environment as a given. We no longer can. We are already changing it in destructive ways. These are difficult issues to think through using terms such as duty or consequence. What duties do we have to nature? What responsibilities do we have to persons not yet in existence? Is an action wrong if it has no significant deleterious effect in itself, but only when combined with many others acting likewise? How shall we assess consequences when the very nature of some of our interventions is such that their results will not be fully known until long after we are no longer here? These quandaries have, if anything, proliferated since Jonas wrote. What responsibility do we bear for global poverty, ignorance and disease when they are the result of policies over which we have no control? What if they are the result of cultural factors whose integrity we feel called on to respect? What are our duties to those suffering from oppression when the oppressors are duly constituted governments of sovereign states? To what extent are we justified in imposing sanctions on evil regimes, when this may exacerbate the sufferings of their people without dislodging the tyrants who were responsible in the first place? Through chaos theory and other insights into ecological systems, we have become familiar with the large and unpredictable effects of relatively small and local disturbances. But this organic view of the interconnectedness of humanity and nature – the guiding metaphor of the global age – makes it exceptionally difficult to establish the parameters of moral decision and action.

Who, in any case, are the actors on the global stage? Throughout the West for the past half century, increasing emphasis has been placed on two institutions: markets and governments. Neither, however, is able to bear the weight currently placed upon it. Markets are by their very nature transactional, not moral. They are about prices, not values. They are arenas of exchange that involve no judgement on what is exchanged, by whom, in return for what. Meanwhile, politics in the West has become ever more procedural and managerial, concerned with delivering maximum public services at minimum cost while bypassing substantive moral questions about what kind of world we seek collectively to make. John Rawls calls this, one of the credos of contemporary liberalism, 'the priority of the right over the good'.[22] Many no longer believe that there is consensus on the common good in societies that have become pluralist and multicultural. Some go further and argue that governments have no right to make collective decisions on the 'good'. That must always be left to individual choice and conscience. One way or another, the two most influential actors – states and markets – have effectively marginalized ethical considerations from their decision-making procedures.

The same is true about the most important newcomer to the international stage: the global corporation. Today, the large multinationals wield enormous power. Of the hundred largest economies today, 51 are corporations and only 49 are nation-states. Several factors make it difficult to integrate them into a coherent policy arena. They exist to make a profit for shareholders. That is their *raison d'être* and logic of decision-making. Wider responsibilities – to the environment, to local cultures and their impact on communities – are not essential to their remit, though many have been forced into it by public pressure and have incorporated it into policies and mission statements. In any case, the sheer mobility of capital and production has meant that they are often able to evade control by nation-states by the simple gambit of moving production elsewhere or factoring it out to local firms, and by moving their financial base to a more congenial country.

There is a human issue as well. In the past there was a living connection between the owners of wealth and its producers. The feudal lord and the industrialist, however exploitative, had at least some interest in the welfare of those they employed. Today's global elites have little connection with the people their decisions affect. They do not live in the same country as those who produce their goods. They may have little if any contact with those who buy them, especially when purchasing is done through the Internet. This is important because moral responsibility is no mere abstraction. It grows out of face-to-face relationships. We see how what we do affects others. That is how we learn what to do and what not to do. The distance and depersonalization of contemporary life have robbed us of the immediate connection between act and consequence, and this too has weakened our moral sense.

An enormous gap has opened up between global elites and others. The global executive is part of an international community. He or she may spend much of the time travelling the world, yet always staying in the same kind of hotel, eating the same sort of food, and dealing with the same sort of people. The vast majority of people, however, even in developed countries, find themselves bound to a locality which has in the meantime been robbed of many of the public spaces and shared activities that once generated community. There is little in common between the extraterritorial elites, for whom physical distance means nothing and time everything, and the others, who often (because of unemployment or part-time employment) have an abundance of time but little freedom to move from place to place.[23] Rarely has there been less to connect decision-makers with those who are affected by what they decide. The operations of the market are no substitute for the sense of overarching moral commonality that links individuals to a shared fate and leads them to think and act for the common good.

The market, in short, has done more than open up extremes of poverty and wealth. It has subverted other institutions – families, communities, the bonds that link members of a society to a common fate, and the moral discourse by which, until now, we were able to maintain a critical distance between 'I want' and 'I ought'. By replacing a hierarchy of collective obligations with a supermarket of personalized lifestyle preferences, it has undermined our ability to talk of public goods – the things (from parks to public services to loyalties) we do not buy or own but share.

* * *

The most unexpected phenomenon in our time, however, has not been the direct effect of globalization but an indirect consequence:

the resurgence of religion as a significant factor in many parts of the world.

If there was one thing on which the architects of Western modernity agreed, it was that organized religion had run its course. Its entire superstructure of beliefs and practices would be replaced by others based on rationality. In the wake of the Reformation, throughout the sixteenth and early seventeenth centuries, Europe had been riven by religious conflict. There were many factors at stake, not all or even most of which were religious. There was the assertion of power by local rulers against the Catholic Church. There was the rise of literacy made possible by the invention of printing. There was a new individualism in the air, the result, in part, of the emergence of a commercial class. To what extent these were the cause or the effect of the rise of Protestantism and Puritanism has been endlessly argued, but the immediate practical consequence was simple. What, when religion gave rise to conflicts it could not resolve, could become the basis of a society no longer united by a single faith? Out of this question modernity was born.

The first and most glittering achievement was science. Descartes had begun his philosophical journey by systematically doubting every received truth. From there it was a short distance to the idea that knowledge should be based on reason and observation, not tradition or authority. Copernicus, Galileo and above all Newton, became the icons of the new epistemology to which all social endeavour ultimately aspired. Experiment would establish truth. Reason would dispel prejudice. Ethics could be constructed on new foundations, whether in human emotion (Hume), rationality (Kant) or the maximization of beneficial consequences (Bentham). Salvation evolved into the new and powerful idea of progress. The American and French revolutions showed that not only knowledge but also politics could be dissociated from religion. Locke's doctrine of toleration led the way to the separation of Church and state and the secularization of politics. Religion might survive in the private places of the soul or the family or the local congregation, but its public role was at an end.

The strange fact was, however, that religion refused to die.

Already in the 1830s a French visitor to the United States, Alexis de Tocqueville, noted its surprising tenacity in the New World. 'Eighteenth-century philosophers', he wrote, 'had a very simple explanation for the gradual weakening of beliefs. Religious zeal, they said, was bound to die down as enlightenment and freedom spread. It is tiresome that the facts do not fit this theory at all.'[24] Much of the rethinking about the contours of the post-Cold War order has recapitulated Tocqueville's discovery. What has emerged is, in George Weigel's phrase, the 'desecularization of the world'.[25]

The most famous of the debates about the future after the fall of the Berlin Wall and the collapse of Soviet communism took place between Francis Fukuyama ('the end of history') and Samuel Huntington ('the clash of civilizations'). Fukuyama's contention was that economics had proved more powerful than politics. The Soviet Union had imploded without a shot being fired because the command economy failed where the market economy succeeded. It had not yielded prosperity, and that is what people wanted. The race, in future, would be to produce video-recorders, not missiles. Economic growth demanded a free market, and thus eventually a free society. Not immediately perhaps, but ultimately, liberal democracy would be the inevitable outcome in one country after another. The ideological struggles of the past were giving way to a Hegelian 'end of history' which might be boring but would at least be peaceful.[26]

Huntington disagreed. Modernization did not mean Westernization. It might well be the case that the politics of the future would no longer be ideological in the twentieth-century sense. But there would still be profound differences and antagonisms between the West and the rest. He called these 'civilizational'. Not every conflict needed to be between nation-states, economic systems or political philosophies. Nor were they likely to be, as they had been in the past, internal wars between contending parties within the West. But history was not moving toward a Hegelian synthesis. Something remained over and above the instrumentalities of production and consumption, power and its distribution. That something was culture, or at its most general level, civilization: the habits of language, history, religion, custom and tradition that divided and would continue to divide humanity. The more international conflict became global, the more it would become civilizational, a clash between ancient but still operative codes of meaning and behaviour.[27]

In retrospect, the most prescient analysis was given by Benjamin Barber in his 1992 essay, 'Jihad vs. McWorld'.[28] For Barber, both tendencies were happening at once. The world was becoming linked into a single interconnected network, driven by technology, ecology, communications and commerce. These very forces, though, were producing their own counter-reaction in the form of 'a threatened Lebanonization of national states in which culture is pitted against culture, people against people, tribe against tribe'. The end of an era in which the conflict between two superpowers dominated all else was leading not to global harmony but the increasing fractiousness of ever smaller groups. 'The planet', he concluded, 'is falling precipitately apart and coming together at the very same moment.'

Few writers have expressed more poignantly than Michael Ignatieff the sense of euphoric expectation that followed the dramatic events of 1989:

> When the Berlin Wall came down, when Václav Havel stood on the balcony in Prague's Wenceslas Square and crowds cheered the collapse of communist regimes across Europe, I thought, like many people, that we were about to witness a new era of liberal democracy ... With blithe lightness of mind, we assumed that the world was moving irrevocably beyond nationalism, beyond tribalism, beyond the provincial confines of the identities inscribed in our passports, toward a global market culture which was to be our new home.[29]

By the end of a journey through conflict zones in Croatia and Serbia, Germany, Ukraine, Quebec, Kurdistan and Northern Ireland, however, his hopes had been shattered. The planet, he now realized:

is not run by sceptics and ironists, but by gunmen and true
believers and the new world they are bequeathing to the
next century already seems a more violent and desperate
place than I could ever have imagined. If I had supposed, as
the Cold War came to an end, that the new world might be
ruled by philosophers and poets, it was because I believed,
foolishly, that the precarious civility and order of the states
in which I live must be what all people rationally desire.
Now I am not so sure. I began the journey as a liberal, and I
end as one, but I cannot help thinking that liberal
civilization – the rule of laws, not men, of argument in
place of force, of compromise in place of violence – runs
deeply against the human grain and is only achieved and
sustained by the most unremitting struggle against human
nature. The liberal virtues – tolerance, compromise, reason
– remain as valuable as ever, but they cannot be preached to
those who are mad with fear or mad with vengeance.[30]

Those words were written in 1993, but they have lost none of their
salience in the intervening years.

* * *

Why has religion returned to the world stage with such elemental
force? There is no single answer, but a broad explanation is not
hard to find. Globalization is profoundly destabilizing. It
epitomizes what Schumpeter called capitalism's 'perennial gale
of creative destruction'.[31] Faced with change, those who feel
threatened by it turn to religion as a source of stability, an
expression of the things that do not change. The global market
tends to reduce all things to economic terms. Religion offers a
different kind of solace. It speaks of the dignity of the person and
the power of the human spirit. It tells us that we are more, or
other, than what we earn or what we buy. In the fast-moving
world economy there are winners and losers. Life takes on a
ruthless, Darwinian struggle for survival. Religion reminds us that
there are other sources of self-worth. We are not necessarily set
against one another in a win-or-lose competition.

Most importantly, no other system does what religion has traditionally undertaken to do, namely to offer an explanation of who we are and why, of our place in the universe and the meaning of events as they unfold around us. The great post-Enlightenment systems – science, economics, and political ideologies – have all retreated from their earlier roles as overarching philosophies. Science has become descriptive, economics transactional, and politics ever more managerial. They tell us what and how but not why. We turn to them to get what we want, but not to know what we ought to want. That is their power, but also, from another perspective, their weakness. Never before have we been faced with more choices, but never before have the great society-shaping institutions offered less guidance on why we should choose this way rather than that. The great metaphors of our time – the supermarket, cable and satellite television and the Internet – put before us a seemingly endless range of options, each offering the great deal, the best buy, the highest specification, the lowest price. But consumption is a poor candidate for salvation. The very happiness we were promised by buying these designer jeans, that watch or this car, is what the next product assures us we do not yet have until we have bought something else. A consumer society is kept going by an endless process of stimulating, satisfying, and re-stimulating desire. It is more like an addiction than a quest for fulfilment.

The twenty-first century has arisen on the ruins of the twentieth, an age in which many of the great political ideologies – fascism, socialism, communism, even nationalism – were discredited. In Fukuyama's vision of the future we sense the return of a hope once expressed in the eighteenth century, that trade would do what politics did not: tame passions, domesticate man the fighter into man the producer and consumer, and lock nations into a win-win network of mutual exchange.[32] The amalgamation of the nation-states of Europe, which had spent the previous centuries in intermittent war, into the European Union seemed to be one augury. The collapse of the Soviet Union was another. What this overlooked, then as now, is that *homo sapiens* is not only, or even primarily, a maximizing animal, choosing rationally between options. We are uniquely a meaning-seeking animal. Our most fundamental questions are Who am I? and To which narrative do I belong? The great hope of the liberal imagination, that politics could be superseded by economics, replacing public good with private choice, was bound to fail because economics as such offers no answer to the big questions of 'Who' and 'Why.' Religion does, and that is its power in the contemporary world. The politics of ideology may have died, but it has been replaced not by 'the end of history' but by the politics of identity.

Religious leaders might be expected to see this as a good thing, and in many ways it is. Religion is an essential element in a human and humane social order, and in the central chapters of this book I will try to say why. But it is precisely now that religious leaders should warn of the dangers ahead. As systems of meaning and purpose, the great world faiths have never been surpassed. As a substitute for politics, however, they are full of danger – and that, in some parts of the world, is what they have become. In some cases, most notably Afghanistan under the Taliban, whole societies have been subjected to the rule of religious law. In others – Saddam Hussein's Iraq is a good example – religion is invoked by essentially secular leaders as a way of mobilizing and directing popular passions. There are some combinations that are incendiary, and the mixture of religion and power is one.

It is worth reminding ourselves of the origins of the words 'politics' and 'religion'. Politics comes from the Greek *polis*, meaning a city. It reminds us of the birthplace of many of our political concepts, namely the Greek city-states, Athens especially, of the pre-Christian centuries. Politics meant the process of governing the basic political unit, the city and its affairs. But cities have another resonance in the classical world. They were where trade took place, where people of different classes and occupations met. The great Mediterranean ports were, by the standards of their time, cosmopolitan. You could meet foreigners there, people who had come in ships to buy and sell or stay and work. In contrast to a village, a city was a place of difference where you could hear many languages and accents and meet people from different faiths and cultures. To this day, politics retains its link with the city as the art of reconciling difference – mediating conflict, adjudicating conflicting claims, providing frameworks of peaceful coexistence. This required a certain set of protocols. We can still hear resonances of the city in words like urbane (*urbs* = a city), civil (*civis* = citizen) and cosmopolitan. Many of the so-called liberal virtues – tolerance, compromise, reason – have their origins in this setting.

The word religion, by contrast, comes from the Latin *religare*, meaning 'to bind'. That is what religions did and still do. They bind people to one another and to God. They form communities. In some cases, as with the great Islamic expansion of the seventh and eighth centuries, or the Holy Roman Empire, those communities may be far larger than nation-states. What they have in common, especially in the case of the great monotheisms, is that they create unities, systems, wholes. They bind the group together through rituals, narratives, collective ceremonies and symbols. Religions, as total systems of meaning, create totalities. They do this in a great variety of ways. There is an enormous difference between the Church of medieval Catholicism, the umma of Islam, the 'priesthood of all believers' of Calvinism and 'the congregation of Israel' of post-biblical Judaism. Religions may create communities which are hierarchical or egalitarian, organic or covenantal. But at their heart is a vision of a unity, an entity, a whole. That is what sets them apart from our mainstream understanding of politics. Difference is where politics lives; but it is what religion transcends. Religion binds. Politics mediates. That is why what, in politics, may be necessary virtues – compromise, ambiguity, diplomacy, coexistence – are, from the point of view of religion, usually seen as vices.

Religion and politics are different enterprises. They arose in response to different needs: in the one case to bind people together in their commonality, in the other to mediate peaceably between their differences. The great tragedies of the twentieth century came when politics was turned into a religion, when the nation (in the case of fascism) or system (communism) was absolutized and turned into a god. The single greatest risk of the twenty-first century is that the opposite may occur: not when politics is religionized but when religion is politicized. What makes religion incapable of being a politics is what led Aristotle to criticize the republic of Plato.[33] Plato in *The Republic* sought to invest the state with the characteristics of a religion. Aristotle replied by saying that without difference there can be no politics. Politics is the space we make for what individual religions seek to overcome – diversity of views, conflicting interests, multiplicity. And whereas once we needed these things at a local level, we now need them globally.

Religions were humanity's first global phenomena. The great faiths of the axial age – especially the monotheisms, Judaism, Christianity and Islam – were born when mankind first lifted its sights beyond the tribe, the city and the nation and thought of humanity as a whole. To this day, more than any other actor on the international stage, they fulfil the twenty-first-century imperative: 'think globally, act locally'. Their vision is global but their setting is local – the congregation, the synagogue, the church, the mosque. The question is: are religions ready for the greatest challenge they have ever faced, namely a world in which even local conflict can have global repercussions? It was one thing for Christians and Muslims to fight one another in the age of the Crusades; quite another to do so in an age of nuclear, chemical and biological weapons. It was one thing for wars of religion to take place on a battlefield, another when anywhere – a plane, a bus, an office-block – can become the frontline and a scene of terror.

Economics can solve economic problems, and politics political ones, but only religion can solve problems that arise out of the religious situation itself. For four centuries the West proceeded on the assumption that science, politics and economics would take the place once held by the Church. The problem of religion would be solved by depriving it of power. What happens, though, when religion returns in all its power – precisely because it answers questions to which science, politics and economics offer no reply? The great faiths provide meaning and purpose for their adherents. The question is: can they make space for those who are not its adherents, who sing a different song, hear a different music, tell a different story? On that question, the fate of the twenty-first century may turn.

43

NOTES

1. Whitehead 1942.
2. Naisbitt and Aburdene 1990.
3. Clinton 2001.
4. Donne 1930, pp. 537-8.
5. Moore and Lewis 1999.
6. See Landes 1998; Jay 2001.
7. Quoted in Barber 2001, p. 130.
8. Hertz 2001, pp. 36-7.
9. Barber 2001, p. 27.
10. Held 2000, p. 175.
11. Gordon Brown, Address to United Nations General Assembly, Special Session on Children, 10 May 2002.
12. Harrison and Huntington 2000, p. xviii.
13. Held and McGrew 2000, pp. 342-3.
14. Hertz 2001, pp. 38-61.
15. Barber 1992.
16. Schumpeter 1947, p. 143.
17. James 1997.
18. Reich 1992 and 2001.
19. MacIntyre 1981, p. 2.
20. Williams 1985.
21. Jonas 1984.
22. Rawls 1993.
23. Bauman 1998.
24. Tocqueville 1968, p. 364.
25. Berger 1999.
26. Fukuyama 1989.
27. Huntington 1996.
28. Barber 1992.
29. Ignatieff 1993, p. 2.
30. Ibid., p. 189.
31. Schumpeter 1947.
32. See Hirschman 1997.
33. Aristotle 1988, p. 1261a: 'So that we ought not to attain this greatest unity even if we could, for it would be the destruction of the state.'

Chapter 3

The Dignity of Difference:
Exorcizing Plato's Ghost

> Politicians at international forums may reiterate a thousand
> times that the basis of the new world order must be universal
> respect for human rights, but it will mean nothing as long as
> this imperative does not derive from respect for the miracle
> of Being ... It must be rooted in self-transcendence:
> transcendence as a hand reaching out to those close to us,
> to foreigners, to the human community, to all living
> creatures, to nature, to the universe; transcendence as a
> deeply and joyously experienced need to be in harmony
> even with what we ourselves are not, with what we do not
> understand, with what seems distant from us in time and
> space, but with which we are mysteriously linked because,
> together with us, all this constitutes a single world;
> transcendence as the only real alternative to extinction.
>
> (Václav Havel, *The Art of the Impossible*)

One belief, more than any other (to quote a phrase of Isaiah
Berlin's)[1] is responsible for the slaughter of individuals on the
altars of the great historical ideals. It is the belief that those who
do not share my faith – or my race or my ideology – do not share
my humanity. At best they are second-class citizens. At worst they
forfeit the sanctity of life itself. They are the unsaved, the
unbelievers, the infidel, the unredeemed; they stand outside the

circle of salvation. If faith is what makes us human, then those who do not share my faith are less than fully human. From this equation flowed the Crusades, the Inquisitions, the jihads, the pogroms, the blood of human sacrifice through the ages. From it – substituting race for faith – ultimately came the Holocaust.

I used to think that the Holocaust had cured us of this idea; that it was impossible not to hear from the ghosts of Auschwitz the cry, 'Never again'. Now I am not so sure. I have come increasingly to the view that if we do not, like Jacob, wrestle with the dark angel of our nature and beliefs, there will be other tragedies. In Rwanda, Cambodia and the Balkans there already have been, and there will be more. This is the greatest religious challenge of all, and much will depend on whether we are equal to it. It is a challenge posed in the Bible's opening chapters. The first recorded act of religious worship leads directly to the first murder, the first fratricide. Two people bring an offering to God. The name of one is Abel; the other was Cain. I read this as a clear and fateful warning, at the very beginning of the book of books, that just as there is a road from faith to redemption, so there is a direct path from religion to violence. What is it that leads people to shed blood in the name of God?

There is one answer with which we are familiar. Religion is about identity, and identity excludes. For every 'We' there is a 'Them', the people not like us. There are kin and non-kin, friends and strangers, brothers and others, and without these boundaries it is questionable whether we would have an identity at all. The sense of belonging goes back to prehistory, to the hunter-gatherer stage in the evolution of mankind, when *homo sapiens* first emerged. Being part of the group was essential to life itself. Outside it, surrounded by predators, the individual could not survive. Some of our deepest, genetically encoded instincts, go back to that time and explain our tendency to form networks, attachments and loyalties. To this day, we call these predispositions *tribal*.

They lie behind some of the earliest religious expressions of mankind. In the pantheon of antiquity there were gods who represented a people or a nation. They watched over its destinies, fought its battles, had their home in a local shrine or sacred mountain, and had, as it were, local jurisdiction. So, for example, the Moabites could see their conflict with the Israelites in terms of a battle between their god, Chemosh, and the God of the Israelites. So primordial is this sense that it never altogether died. It revived in secular terms in the romantic nationalism of nineteenth-century Europe in ideas such as the *Volksgeist*, the 'spirit of the race' conceived in terms no less mystical than its pagan predecessors. It survives today in football grounds and sporting contests throughout the world.

Tribalism has immense power, as anyone who has ever been caught up in the emotions of a crowd can testify. To surrender the lonely self to something larger, more powerful and elemental, is one of the deepest instincts of mankind. A tribal world is agonistic: a place of conflict where the strongest wins and honour and glory lie in fighting, even dying, in a noble cause. That was the mood among many young men as they set off in 1914 to fight for king and country in the First World War.[2] It took millions of deaths, a further world war, and the awesome power of atomic and nuclear weapons, before the West reached the collective conclusion that the price of war was too high.

Today we are inclined to see resurgent tribalism as the great danger of our fragmenting world. It is, but it is not the only danger. The paradox is that the very thing we take to be the antithesis of tribalism – universalism – can also be deeply threatening, and may be equally inadequate as an account of the human situation. A global culture is a universal culture, and universal cultures, though they have brought about great good, have also done immense harm. They see as the basis of our humanity the fact that we are all ultimately the same. We are vulnerable. We are embodied creatures. We feel hunger, thirst, fear, pain. We reason, hope, dream, aspire. These things are all true and important. But we are also different. Each landscape, language, culture, community is unique. Our very dignity as persons is rooted in the fact that none of us – not even genetically identical twins – is exactly like any other. Therefore none of us is replaceable, substitutable, a mere instance of a type. That is what makes us persons, not merely organisms or machines. If our commonalities are all that ultimately matter, then our differences are distractions to be overcome.

This view, I will argue, is profoundly mistaken. It is a mistake that has been made several times in the history of the West, and we are in the process of making it again in the form of globalization. Nothing else I have to say in this book will be more radical or harder to understand, because it challenges an assumption that for at least two millennia has been at the heart of Western civilization. Yet that is the case I will make: that we need nothing less than a paradigm shift in our understanding of our commonalities and differences. It may seem bizarre to suggest a connection between the tragedy of September 11 and a Greek philosopher who lived almost 2,500 years ago, but that is what I am going to suggest. I call it Plato's ghost, and it has haunted the Western imagination ever since.

* * *

In the Stanza della Segnatura in the Vatican hangs one of the supreme artistic achievements of the Renaissance: Raphael's vast canvas, the *School at Athens*. Framing the scene and dominating the upper half of the painting are the magnificent columns, statues and arches of the academy through one of which, in the far distance, can be seen a blue and lightly clouded sky. Occupying the centre and foreground are the members of the academy in small groups, speaking, listening, arguing, gesticulating and disputing. In the front, one solitary thinker sits on the steps wrapped in thought, head on hand like Rodin's *Penseur*. Our eyes are drawn, however, to the two figures in the middle, the two giants of Greek thought. On the left is Plato, his hair and beard white with age, and next to him a younger man, Aristotle, who will become his most famous disciple and whose influence will at times outshine that of the master himself. Aristotle's left hand is turned downward, but Plato's right hand is raised in an upward-pointing gesture.

We need no caption to tell us what Plato is saying:

If you seek truth, Aristotle, do not look down to this world
that surrounds us, empirical reality with all its messy and
chaotic particulars. Look up to heaven and the world of
forms, for it is there that you will find the true essence and
nature of things. There, in place of particularity and
conflict, you will find unity and harmony.

In the world of ideas, difference is resolved into sameness.
Particulars give way to universals. The world we see, in which we
move and live, he argued in *The Republic* in the famous parable of
the cave, is a mere play of shadows.[3] The true essence of things is
not matter but form, ideas, not their concrete embodiment in the
world of the senses. That is where trees become Treeness, where
men become Man and apparent truths coalesce into Truth.

It is a wondrous dream, that of Plato, and one that has never
ceased to appeal to his philosophical and religious heirs: the
dream of reason, a world of order set against the chaos of life, an
eternity beyond the here and now. Its single most powerful idea is
that truth – reality, the essence of things – is universal. How could
it be otherwise? What is true is true for everyone at all times, and
so the more universal a culture is, the closer to truth it comes. Is
that not, after all, how we grow to maturity as individuals? We
begin, in childhood, by being attached to our immediate family.
Then, as our exposure to the world widens, we come successively
to embrace friends, neighbours, the community, society and
eventually all mankind. So it is with civilization itself. The history
of *homo sapiens* is precisely the move from small, roving bands to
tribes, city-states, nations and ultimately, if not yet, global
governance. Particularity – the world of the senses and the
passions – is the source of conflict, prejudice, error and war.
Universality is the realm of truth, harmony and peace. The move
from primitive to sophisticated, parochial to cosmopolitan, local
to global, is the journey from particular attachments to universal
reason.

Seen through this set of values, Judaism cannot but be seen as a
revolution that reached half-way. It stands between two eras: that
of the tribal cultures and local deities of the ancient world on the

one hand, and on the other the universalistic cultures such as those of Greece and Rome, and their religious successors, Christianity and Islam. Judaism was, as it were, born *in media res*. It was able to conceive of a universal God, but not yet of a universal faith. Here and there in its sacred texts there appeared shafts of light in the form of the universalistic visions of Amos and Isaiah, but Judaism remained a particularistic and therefore tribal faith. It was trapped into the parochialism of antiquity.

This view is a travesty, but were it no more than that I would not trouble to argue the case here. My argument is far more fundamental, namely that universalism is an inadequate response to tribalism, and no less dangerous. It leads to the belief – superficially compelling but quite false – that there is only one truth about the essentials of the human condition, and it holds true for all people at all times. If I am right, you are wrong. If what I believe is the truth, then your belief, which differs from mine, must be an error from which you must be converted, cured and saved. From this flowed some of the great crimes of history, some under religious auspices, others – the French and Russian revolutions, for example – under the banner of secular philosophies, but both under the enchantment of Plato's ghost.[4]

* * *

The Hebrew Bible is a book whose strangeness is little understood. It tells the story of God who makes a covenant with an individual, Abraham, whose children become a family, then a tribe, then a collection of tribes, then a nation. It is the narrative of a particular people. Yet the Bible does not begin with this people. Instead it starts by telling a story about humanity as a whole. Its first eleven chapters are about Adam and Eve, Cain and Abel, Noah and the Flood, Babel and its tower – archetypes of humanity as a whole. This is not simply an etiological myth, a tale of origins. It is quite clearly intended to be more than that. The Bible is doing here what it does elsewhere, namely conveying a set of truths through narrative. But by any conventional standard, the order of these stories is precisely wrong. They *begin* with universal humanity and only then proceed to the particular: one man, Abraham, one woman, Sarah, and one people, their descendants. *By reversing the normal order, and charting, instead, a journey from the universal to the particular, the Bible represents the great anti-Platonic narrative in Western civilization.*

Against Plato and his followers, the Bible argues that universalism is the first, not the last, phase in the growth of the moral imagination. The world of the first eleven chapters of Genesis is global, a monoculture ('the whole world had one language and a common speech'). It is to this world that God first speaks. He gives Adam a command, Cain a warning, Noah His grace. Yet, one by one these experiments fail. Adam disobeys. Cain becomes a murderer. Noah inhabits a world filled with violence. A poignant verse speaks of God's disappointment: 'The Lord regretted that He had made man on earth and His heart was filled with pain' (6: 6). After the Flood, God makes a covenant with all mankind, the first universal moral code. But that is not the end of the story. There then follows a brief passage that deserves to become a parable of our time:

> Now the whole world had one language and a common speech. As men moved eastwards, they found a plain in Shinar and settled there.
>
> They said to each other, 'Come, let's make bricks and bake them thoroughly.' They used brick instead of stone, and tar instead of mortar. Then they said, 'Come, let us build ourselves a city, with a tower that reaches to the heavens, so that we may make a name for ourselves and not be scattered over the face of the whole earth.'
>
> But the Lord came down to see the city and the tower that the men were building. The Lord said, 'If as one people speaking the same language they have begun to do this, then nothing they plan to do will be impossible for them. Come, let us go down and confuse their language so that they will not understand each other.'
>
> So the Lord scattered them from there over all the earth, and they stopped building the city. That is why it was called Babel – because there the Lord confused the language of the

whole world. From there the Lord scattered them over the face of the whole earth. (Genesis 11: 1–9)

The men on the plain at Shinar make a technological discovery. They learn how to make bricks by drying clay – the first processed (as opposed to entirely natural) building material in history. As after so many other technological advances, they immediately conclude that they now have the power of gods. They are no longer subject to nature. They have become its masters. They will storm the heavens. Their man-made environment – the city with its ziggurat or artificial mountain – will replicate the structure of the cosmos, but here they will rule, not God. It is a supreme act of hubris, committed time and again in history – from the Sumerian city-states, to Plato's *Republic*, to empires, ancient and modern, to the Soviet Union. It is *the attempt to impose a man-made unity on divinely created diversity*. That is what is wrong with universalism.

Babel – the first global project – is the turning point in the biblical narrative. From then on, God will not attempt a universal order again until the end of days. Babel ends with the division of mankind into a multiplicity of languages, cultures, nations and civilizations. God's covenant with humanity as a whole has not ceased. But from here on he will focus on one family, and eventually one people, to be his witnesses and bearers of his covenant – a people in whose history his presence will be peculiarly transparent. He will ask of them that they be willing to give up home, birthplace and land, all the familiar certainties, and undertake a journey with God as their only protection. Theirs will be a singular and exemplary fate. They will be a people who are different. Indeed the word *kadosh*, 'holy', in the Bible means just that – being different, set apart, distinctive. The question is, Why?

* * *

Judaism has a structural peculiarity so perplexing and profound that though its two daughter monotheisms, Christianity and Islam, took much else from it, they did not adopt this: Judaism is a particularist monotheism. It believes in one God but not in one religion, one culture, one truth. *The God of Abraham is the God of all mankind, but the faith of Abraham is not the faith of all mankind.* There is no equivalent in Judaism to the doctrine that *extra ecclesiam non est salus*, 'outside the Church there is no salvation'. On the contrary, Judaism's ancient sages maintained that 'the pious of the nations have a share in the world to come'.[5] Indeed, the Bible takes it for granted that the God of Israel is not only the God of Israel. He is also the God of Abraham's contemporary, Melchizedek, king of Salem, not a member of the covenantal family but still a 'priest of the Most High God'. He is acknowledged by Jethro, Moses' father-in-law and a Midianite priest, who gives Israel its first lesson in government – the appointment of heads of thousands, hundreds, fifties and tens. Two of the Bible's heroic women, Tamar and Ruth, are not Israelites. The first is a Canaanite, the second a Moabite, yet each has a place of honour in Israel's history and both are ancestors of its greatest king, David. How does such an idea arise and what does it imply?

To this I suggest a radical answer. God, the creator of humanity, having made a covenant with all humanity, then turns to one people and commands it to be different *in order to teach humanity the dignity of difference*. Biblical monotheism is not the idea that there is one God and therefore one truth, one faith, one way of life. On the contrary, it is the idea that *unity creates diversity*. That is the non-Platonic miracle of creation. What is real, remarkable and the proper object of our wonder is not the quintessential leaf but the 250,000 different kinds there actually are; not the idea of a bird but the 9,000 species that exist today; not the metalanguage that embraces all others, but the 6,000 languages still spoken throughout the world. Thanks to our new-found knowledge of DNA we now know that all life in its astonishing complexity had a single origin. Matt Ridley puts it breathlessly but well:

> The three-letter words of the genetic code are the same in every creature. CGA means arginine and GCG means alanine – in bats, in beetles, in bacteria. They even mean the same in the misleadingly named archaebacteria living at

boiling temperatures in sulphurous springs thousands of feet beneath the surface of the Atlantic ocean or in those microscopic capsules of deviousness called viruses. Wherever you go in the world, whatever animal, plant, bug or blob you look at, if it is alive, it will use the same dictionary and know the same code. All life is one. The genetic code, bar a few tiny local aberrations, mostly for unexplained reasons in the ciliate protozoa, is the same in every creature. We all use exactly the same language. This means – and religious people might find this a useful argument – that there was only one creation, one single event when life was born.[6]

Judaism is about the miracle of unity that creates diversity.

The essential message of the Book of Genesis is that universality – the covenant with Noah – is only the context of and prelude to the irreducible multiplicity of cultures, those systems of meaning by which human beings have sought to understand their relationship to one another, the world and the source of being. Plato's assertion of the universality of truth is valid when applied to science and the description of what is. It is invalid when applied to ethics, spirituality and our sense of what ought to be. There is a difference between *physis* and *nomos*, description and prescription, nature and culture, or – to put it in biblical terms – between creation and revelation. Cultures are like languages. The world they describe is the same but the ways they do so are almost infinitely varied. English is not French. Italian is not German. Urdu is not Ugaritic. Each language is the product of a specific community and its history, its shared experiences and sensibilities. There is no universal language. There is no way we can speak, communicate or even think without placing ourselves within the constraints of a particular language whose contours were shaped by hundreds of generations of speakers, storytellers, artists and visionaries who came before us, whose legacy we inherit and of whose story we become a part. Within any language we can say something new. No language is fixed, unalterable, complete. What we cannot do is place ourselves outside the particularities of language to arrive at a truth, a way of understanding and responding to the world that applies to everyone at all times. That is not the essence of humanity but an attempt to escape from humanity.

The same applies to religion. The radical transcendence of God in the Hebrew Bible means nothing more or less than that *there is a difference between God and religion.* God is universal, religions are particular. Religion is the translation of God into a particular language and thus into the life of a group, a nation, a community of faith. In the course of history, God has spoken to mankind in many languages: through Judaism to Jews, Christianity to Christians, Islam to Muslims. Only such a God is truly transcendental – greater not only than the natural universe but also than the spiritual universe articulated in any single faith, any specific language of human sensibility. How could a sacred text convey such an idea? It would declare that *God is God of all humanity, but no single faith is or should be the faith of all humanity.* Only such a narrative would lead us to see the presence of God in people of other faiths. Only such a worldview could reconcile the particularity of cultures with the universality of the human condition.

This means that religious truth is not universal. What it does *not* mean is that it is relative. There is a difference, all too often ignored, between absoluteness and universality. I have an absolute obligation to my child, but it is not a universal one. Indeed it is precisely this non-universality, this particularity, that constitutes parenthood – the ability to feel a bond with *this* child, not to all children indiscriminately. That is what makes love, love: not a generalized affection for persons of such-and-such a type, but a particular attachment to this person in his or her uniqueness. This ability to form an absolute bond of loyalty and obligation to someone in particular as opposed to persons-in-general goes to the very core of what we mean by being human. It is the theme explored by Steven Spielberg in his film *AI*. In it, a couple whose son is in a coma acquire a child-robot that has been programmed to love. The question is whether they can return that love, knowing that he/it is one of a type taken from a production line of dozens of identical products. The answer given by the film is that they cannot, which is almost certainly true and a reason why we should never go down the road of reproductive cloning or anything else that threatens to reduce persons to types. The essential irreplaceability of persons is what gives love its vulnerability, its openness to loss and grief, its fragility and pathos. It is what separates science (the search for universals) from poetry (the love of particulars). It is also what distinguishes the God of the philosophers from the God of the Hebrew Bible.

God as we encounter Him in the Bible is not a philosophical or scientific concept: the first cause, the prime mover, initiator of the Big Bang. He is a parent, sometimes male ('Have we not all one father?'), sometimes female ('Like one whom his mother comforts, so will I comfort you'), but always bearing the love that a parent feels for a child he/she has brought into being. The God of the Hebrew Bible is not a Platonist, loving the abstract form of humanity. He is a particularist, loving each of his children for what they are: Isaac *and* Ishmael, Jacob *and* Esau, Israel *and* the nations, choosing one for a particular destiny, to be sure, but blessing the others, each in their own way.[7] The God of Abraham teaches humanity a more complex truth than simple oppositions – particular/universal, individual/state, tribe/humanity – would allow. We are particular *and* universal, the same *and* different, human beings as such, *but also* members of this family, that community, this history, that heritage. Our particularity is our window on to universality, just as our language is the only way we have of understanding the world we share with speakers of other languages. God no more wants all faiths and cultures to be the same than a loving parent wants his or her children to be the same. That is the conceptual link between love, creation and difference. We serve God, author of diversity, by respecting diversity.

* * *

This gives biblical ethics a different character from philosophical ethics. Philosophical ethics, true to its Platonic origins, focuses on what we have in common: rationality (Kant), emotion (Hume), or our desire for pleasure and aversion to pain (Bentham). Duty, obligation, sympathy, solidarity – these are the things we share in virtue of our universality. They belong to Man, not men; Humanity, not individual human beings; the unity of the moral world, not its diversity. Even when philosophy focuses on the individual it tends to do so in abstract terms: the 'unsituated self' divorced from constitutive attachments to family, friends, community and history.[8] That is what gives philosophical morality its 'thin' or context-free character.

Biblical morality, by contrast, is far more complex. It emphasizes the dual nature of our moral situation. On the one hand, we are members of the universal human family and thus of the (Noahide) covenant with all mankind. There are indeed moral universals – the sanctity of life, the dignity of the human person, the right to be free, to be no man's slave or the object of someone else's violence. The three vignettes of Moses' life before he becomes leader of the Israelites perfectly illustrate this. He intervenes, first to rescue an Israelite from an Egyptian; then an Israelite from a fellow Israelite; then the (non-Israelite) daughters of Jethro from (non-Israelite) shepherds who are preventing them from watering their flock. Moses recognizes the universal character of injustice and fights against it, regardless of who is perpetrating it and who is its victim.

On the other hand, we are also members of a particular family with its specific history and memory. We are part of a 'thick' or context-bound morality (represented, in Judaism, by the Abrahamic and Mosaic covenants) which confers on us loyalties and obligations to the members of our community that go beyond mere justice. We have duties to our parents and children, friends and neighbours, and the members of society considered as an extended family ('When your brother becomes poor …'). The generic word for such duties is *chessed*, usually translated as 'kindness', but meaning the loving obligations we owe to those with whom we are linked in a covenantal bond. It is precisely these moral intimacies that give life to the families and communities in which we learn the grammar and syntax of reciprocity and altruism. Michael Walzer explains why it is that 'thick' or context-laden moralities are more fundamental than 'thin' or universal ones:

Societies are necessarily particular because they have members and memories, members with memories not only of their own but also of their common life. Humanity, by contrast, has members but no memory, and so it has no history and no culture, no customary practices, no familiar life-ways, no festivals, no shared understanding of social goods. It is human to have such things, but there is no singular human way of having them. At the same time, the members of all the different societies, because they are human, can acknowledge each other's different ways, respond to each other's cries for help, learn from each other, and march (sometimes) in each other's parades.[9]

The universality of moral concern is not something we learn by being universal but by being particular. Because we know what it is to be a parent, loving our children, not children in general, we understand what it is for someone else, somewhere else, to be a parent, loving his or her children, not ours. There is no road to human solidarity that does not begin with moral particularity – by coming to know what it means to be a child, a parent, a neighbour, a friend. We learn to love humanity by loving specific human beings. There is no short-cut.[10]

* * *

Nowhere is the singularity of biblical ethics more evident than in its treatment of the issue that has proved to be the most difficult in the history of human interaction, namely *the problem of the stranger*, the one who is not like us. Most societies at most times have been suspicious of, and aggressive toward, strangers. That is understandable, even natural. Strangers are non-kin. They come from beyond the tribe. They stand outside the network of reciprocity that creates and sustains communities. That is what makes the Mosaic books unusual in the history of moral thought. As the rabbis noted, the Hebrew Bible in one verse commands, 'You shall love your neighbour as yourself', but in no fewer than 36 places commands us to 'love the stranger'.

Time and again it returns to this theme:

You shall not oppress a stranger, for you know the heart of the stranger – you yourselves were strangers in the land of Egypt.[11]

When a stranger lives with you in your land, do not ill-treat him. The stranger who lives with you shall be treated like the native-born. Love him as yourself, for you were strangers in the land of Egypt. I am the Lord your God.[12]

It does not assume that this is easy or instinctive. It does not derive it from reason or emotion alone, knowing that under stress, these have rarely been sufficient to counter the human tendency to *dis*like the *un*like and exclude people not like us from our radius of moral concern. Instead it speaks of history: 'You know what it is like to be different, because there was a time when you, too, were persecuted for being different.'

Indeed, it is hard to avoid the conclusion that this is precisely the reason why the Israelites have to undergo exile and slavery prior to their birth as a nation. They have to learn from the inside and never lose the memory of what it feels like to be an outsider, an alien, a stranger. It is their formative experience, re-enacted every year in the drama of Passover – as if to say that only those who know what it is to be slaves, understand at the core of their being why it is wrong to enslave others. Only those who have felt the loneliness of being a stranger find it natural to identify with strangers. Even Moses, who grew up as an Egyptian prince, suffers his own exile in Midian and calls his first son Gershom ('there I was a stranger'), saying, 'I have been a stranger in a strange land.'

We encounter God in the face of a stranger. That, I believe, is the Hebrew Bible's single greatest and most counterintuitive contribution to ethics. God creates difference; therefore it is in one-who-is-different that we meet God. Abraham encounters God when he invites three strangers into his tent. Jacob meets God when he wrestles with an unnamed adversary alone at night. The Book of Ruth, which tells the prehistory of David, Israel's greatest king, reaches its climax when Ruth says to Boaz (her 'redeemer'), 'Why have I found favour in your eyes such that you recognize me, though I am a stranger' (2: 10). The human other is a trace of the Divine Other. As an ancient Jewish teaching puts it: 'When a human being makes many coins in the same mint, they all come out the same. God makes every person in the same image – His image – and each is different.'[13] The supreme religious challenge is to see God's image in one who is not in our image. That is the converse of tribalism. But it is also something other than universalism. It takes difference seriously. It recognizes the integrity of other cultures, other civilizations, other paths to the presence of God. The prophet Malachi says to the Israelites, 'From furthest east to furthest west my name is great among the nations, says the Lord of Hosts, but you profane it . . .' (1: 10). The God of Israel is larger than the faith of Israel. Traces of his presence can be found throughout the world. We do not have to share a creed or code to be partners in the covenant of mankind. The prophets of Israel wrestle with an idea still counterintuitive to the Platonic mind: that moral and spiritual dignity extend far beyond the boundaries of any one civilization. They belong to the other, the outsider, the stranger, the one who does not fit our system, race or creed.

* * *

We can now state what Judaism represents in the history of Western thought. The story of the covenantal people begins with two journeys: Abraham and Sarah's from Mesopotamia, and Moses and the Israelites' from Egypt. Mesopotamia in the days of Abraham and Egypt in the age of Moses were the supreme economic and political powers of their time. *Judaism was born as a protest against empires, because imperialism and its latter-day successors, totalitarianism and fundamentalism, are attempts to impose a single truth on a plural world*, to reduce men to Man, cultures to a single culture, to eliminate diversity in the name of a single sociopolitical order.

The faith of Israel declares the oneness of God and the plurality of man. It moves beyond both tribalism and its antithesis, universalism. Tribalism and its modern counterpart, nationalism, assumes there is one god (or 'spirit' or 'race' or 'character') for each nation. Universalism contends that there is one God – and therefore one truth, one way, one creed – for all humanity. Neither does justice to the human other, the stranger who is not in my image but is nevertheless in God's image. Tribalism denies rights to the outsider. Universalism grants rights if and only if the outsider converts, conforms, assimilates, and thus ceases to be an outsider. Tribalism turns the concept of a chosen people into that of a master-race. Universalism turns the truth of a single culture into the measure of humanity. The results are often tragic and always an affront to human dignity.

Not all empires are universalist. The Ottoman Empire, for example, preserved a significant measure of local autonomy for the various cultures and faith groups under its aegis. There have been five universalist cultures in the history of the West: the Alexandrian Empire, ancient Rome, medieval Christianity and Islam, and the Enlightenment. Jews suffered under all five. What is particularly significant is that three – Greece, Rome and the Enlightenment – prided themselves on their tolerance. Like certain forms of tolerance today ('political correctness' comes to mind), it turned out to be highly circumscribed. Antiochus IV banned the public practice of Judaism. The Romans destroyed the Temple. The Enlightenment failed to prevent the Holocaust. What turned out to be the source of intolerance was not religion as such – three of the five civilizations were, after all, not religious. Rather, it was universalism or what I have called 'Plato's ghost'. The critical test of any order is: does it make space for otherness? Does it acknowledge the dignity of difference?

That has now become a, perhaps *the*, central question of the global age. Difference has now become part of the texture of daily life. At work, in the street and on the television screen, we are regularly confronted with people whose faith, culture, accent, race, skin colour and customs are unlike ours. That can be an enriching experience or a threatening one. As Benjamin Barber pointed out, there are centripetal and centrifugal forces at work – on the one hand McWorld, a largely American culture conveyed by multinational corporations, branded goods, media stars, cable and satellite television and the Internet, and on the other a resurgent tribalism that rejects Western 'decadence' and reasserts primordial identities, some religious, some ethnic, often a combination of both. When the two meet and collide, as they did on September 11, the world trembles. To hold the two in balance, to recognize and give due weight to our commonalities and differences, the universal and the particular, is one of the hardest of all cultural and spiritual challenges but it is the only way to avoid a clash of civilizations – and what is at risk in that clash grows yearly.

After 1945, the world placed its faith – as did the French Revolution – in a universal code of human rights. That is our contemporary equivalent of the biblical covenant with Noah. There is much to be said for this, but it is only half of what is needed for the coexistence of diverse cultures. No universal code as such tells us what we would lose were the multiplicity of civilizations to be reduced; were one culture to dominate all others; were distinctive voices to be lost from the conversation of mankind. The abstract language of rights fails to enter into the depth of what Hinduism means to a Hindu, or Confucianism to its devotees. It suggests that the particularities of a culture are mere accretions to our essential and indivisible humanity, instead of being the very substance of how most people learn what it is to be human. In particular, it understates the difficulty and necessity of making space for strangers – the very thing that has been the source of racism and exclusion in almost every society known to history. If we are to live in close proximity to difference, as in a global age we do, we will need more than a code of rights, more even than mere tolerance. We will need to understand that just as the natural environment depends on biodiversity, so the human environment depends on cultural diversity, because no one creed has a monopoly on spiritual truth; no one civilization encompasses all the spiritual, ethical and artistic expressions of mankind.

* * *

In 1981 Isaiah Berlin wrote some notes for a friend who was about to deliver a lecture and turned to him for help. Berlin was due to go abroad the next day and wrote the following hurried notes, which convey, as well as anything he wrote, his lifelong opposition to intolerance and what he believed to be its source:

> Few things have done more harm than the belief on the part of individuals and groups (or tribes or states or nations or churches) that he or she or they are in *sole* possession of the truth ... It is a terrible and dangerous arrogance to believe that you alone are right: have a magical eye which sees *the* truth: and that others cannot be right if they disagree. This makes one certain that there is *one* goal and only one for one's nation or church or the whole of humanity, and that it is worth any amount of suffering (particularly on the part of other people) if only the goal is attained – 'through an ocean of blood to the Kingdom of Love' (or something like this) said Robespierre: and Hitler, Lenin, Stalin, and I daresay leaders in the religious wars of Christian v. Muslim or Catholics v. Protestants sincerely believed this: the belief that there is one and only one true answer to the central questions which have agonized mankind and that one has it oneself – or one's Leader has it – was responsible for the oceans of blood: But no Kingdom of Love sprang from it – or could ...[14]

Shortly before he died, in 1997, he asked that I should officiate at his funeral. In the tribute I paid to him, I quoted one of the most haunting of the sayings of the Jewish sages – a story they told about the creation of mankind. Although at least fifteen hundred years old, it seemed to me to say what he had spent much of his life teaching:

> Rabbi Shimon said: When God was about to create Adam, the ministering angels split into contending groups. Some said, 'Let him be created.' Others said, 'Let him not be created.' That is why it is written: 'Mercy and truth collided, righteousness and peace clashed' (Psalm 85: 11).
>
> Mercy said, 'Let him be created, because he will do merciful deeds.'

Truth said, 'Let him not be created, for he will be full of falsehood.'

Righteousness said, 'Let him be created, for he will do righteous deeds.'

Peace said, 'Let him not be created, for he will never cease quarrelling.'

What did the Holy One, blessed be He, do? He took truth and threw it to the ground.

The angels said, 'Sovereign of the universe, why do You do thus to Your own seal, truth? Let truth arise from the ground.'

Thus it is written, 'Let truth spring up from the earth' (Psalm 85: 12).[15]

This is an audacious theological interpretation. God, it suggests, was in two minds before creating mankind. Yes, humanity is capable of great acts of altruism and self-sacrifice, but it is also constantly at war. Human beings tell lies and are full of strife. God takes truth and throws it to the ground, meaning: for life to be livable, truth on earth cannot be what it is in heaven. Truth in heaven may be platonic – eternal, harmonious, radiant. But man cannot aspire to such truth, and if he does, he will create conflict not peace. Men kill because they believe they possess the truth while their opponents are in error. In that case, says God, throwing truth to the ground, let human beings live by a different standard of truth, one that is human and thus conscious of its limitations. Truth on the ground is multiple, partial. Fragments of it lie everywhere. Each person, culture and language has part of it; none has it all.

Truth on earth is not, nor can it aspire to be, the whole truth. It is limited, not comprehensive; particular, not universal. When two propositions conflict it is not necessarily because one is true the other false. It may be, and often is, that each represents a different perspective on reality, an alternative way of structuring order, no more and no less commensurable than a Shakespeare sonnet, a Michelangelo painting or a Schubert sonata. In heaven there is truth; on earth there are truths. Therefore, each culture has something to contribute. Each person knows something no one else does. The sages said: 'Who is wise? One who learns from all men.'[16] The wisest is not one who knows himself wiser than others: he is one who knows all men have some share of the truth, and is willing to learn from them, for none of us knows all the truth and each of us knows some of it.

Nothing has proved harder in the history of civilization than to see God, or good, or human dignity in those whose language is not mine, whose skin is a different colour, whose faith is not my faith and whose truth is not my truth. There are, surely, many ways of arriving at this generosity of spirit, and each faith must find its own. The way I have discovered, having listened to Judaism's sacred texts in the context of the tragedies of the twentieth century and the insecurities of the twenty-first, is that the truth at the beating heart of monotheism is that God is greater than religion; that He is only partially comprehended by any faith. He is my God, but also your God. He is on my side, but also on your side. He exists not only in my faith, but also in yours. That is not to say that there are many gods. That is polytheism. Nor is it to say that God endorses every act done in His name. On the contrary: a God of your side as well as mine must be a God of justice who stands above us both, teaching us to make space for one another, to hear each other's claims and to resolve them equitably. Only such a God would be truly transcendent – greater not only than the natural universe but also than the spiritual universe capable of being comprehended in any one language, any single faith. Only such a God could teach mankind to make peace other than by conquest and conversion, and as something nobler than practical necessity.

What would faith be like? It would be like being secure in one's home, yet moved by the beauty of foreign places, knowing that they are someone else's home, not mine, but still part of the glory of the world that is ours. It would be like being fluent in English, yet thrilled by the rhythms and resonances of an Italian sonnet one only partially understands. It would be to know that I am a sentence in the story of my people and its faith, but that there are other stories, each written by God out of the letters of lives bound

of Seattle and elsewhere have turned out to be not local incidents but the first tremors of an earthquake, a seismic shift in the global mood. We have moved into one of the most dangerous of all environments: the politics of insecurity.

I want, in this chapter, to understand the nature of this insecurity, because it is this, more than anything, that gives rise to political and religious extremism and to the kind of authoritarian populism that threatens free societies. In part, it has to do with the sheer pace of the technological, cultural and economic transformations through which we are living. But this cannot be all. The nineteenth century was also a time of immense change. Industrialization, the development of railways and the growth of trade brought about wrenching alterations in people's lives. There was a movement of populations from the countryside to towns. Work moved from home to factory. Writers from Dickens to Disraeli spoke of child labour, poverty, the bleak urban landscape and new forms of social division (Disraeli's 'two nations'). Urban crime was so widespread that it was unsafe to walk city streets at night. Yet these problems, though they gave rise to social criticism and political activism, did not generate the kind of uncertainty we feel today. In Britain, at any rate, the Victorian era was a time without revolution. It was, in ways that seem remote to us now, an age of confidence. What is it about our present situation that is so anxiety-creating and destabilizing?

One factor is clear: the changes through which we have lived have been the most rapid and dramatic in the history of mankind. The twentieth century alone saw technical advance at a rate that has no precedent. When it began there had still been no successful attempt at one of mankind's oldest dreams: powered flight. That dates to the Wright brothers in 1903. There had been no transatlantic radio transmission. That we owe to Marconi in 1901. Today space shuttles are routine and we can communicate instantly across the world. A single century saw the birth of television, the computer, the Internet, the laser beam, the credit card, artificial intelligence, satellite communication, organ transplantation and microsurgery. Journeys that a lifetime ago would have taken months today take hours. We have sent space probes to distant planets, photographed the birth of galaxies, fathomed the origins of the universe and decoded the biological structures of life itself. The frontiers of human possibility extend daily.

The pace of change continues to accelerate. Barring catastrophes like the meteorite which crashed into the planet 65 million years ago, bringing the age of dinosaurs to an end, the process of evolution is, in human terms, achingly slow, a matter of tens of millions of years. Stephen Jay Gould has argued that there have been long periods of stasis followed by relatively short ones of change: he calls his model punctuated equilibrium. What early on singled out *homo sapiens* from other species was the degree to which his behaviour was passed on across the generations not by genes but by culture, allowing for much more rapid and conscious adaptation to environmental and other kinds of change. We are, *par excellence*, the learning animal. Even so, the development of tools and technologies was initially slow. It has been estimated that the average rate of innovation during the Middle Paleolithic era was one new discovery every 20,000 years. That quickened in the Upper Paleolithic age to one in 1,400 years, and in the Mesolithic (from 10,000 BCE onwards) it became one every 200 years.[1] The significance of this prehistory is that it is when many of our instinctual behaviour patterns were formed. Adaptive we may be, but we are not made for constant, relentless alterations in our living conditions.

That is what we now face at ever-increasing speed. It took 38 years for radio to reach 50 million users in the United States. In the case of computers it took sixteen years. The Internet reached 50 million users in four years. Computer power doubles every eighteen months and shows no sign of slackening. The Internet doubles every year. The number of DNA sequences we can analyse doubles every two years. A huge gap has opened up between the transformations happening around us and our ability to respond. Early in the twentieth century, William Ogburn coined the concept of 'cultural lag'[2] – a state, like now, in which material culture, such as technology, is being transformed faster than *non*-material culture such as modes of governance and social norms. When the world out there is changing faster than the world in here – in our mental and emotional responses – our environment becomes bewildering and threatening. Societies take time to change. So do people.

In 1994 I was making a television documentary about the family. During the course of my research I came across a woman who had developed a pioneering approach to the cure of stammering among young children. She was using the family as a therapeutic unit. Her view was that dysfunctional behaviour was often reinforced by family relationships, and that if she was to cure the children she had to work with the parents as well. As part of her programme she asked the parents to think of the most precious object they owned. For some it was a wedding ring, for others a family heirloom, but for all of them it was an item invested with deep emotional attachment. Then she told them to imagine losing it, and asked them to describe their responses. They varied from panic and shock to deep sadness and bereavement. Then she said: 'Now you know what it will feel like for your child to lose its stammer.'

It was a moment of utter bewilderment. Until then the parents had all assumed that their child wanted to be able to speak normally. Their stammer impeded the child's social life. It made things difficult at school or among friends. It was, in short, a dysfunction. What the therapist wanted the parents to understand is that a dysfunction can sometimes be less fearful than change itself. We get used to our disabilities and build them into our relationships. They become familiar, part of our world, integral to our self-image, and the hardest thing can be to let go. Change, even change for the better, can be disorienting, threatening, traumatic. That is why the twenty-first century, with its non-stop transformations, will be deeply unsettling.

* * *

But this is only part of the story. Another, more significant factor, is the breakdown of the institutions of social life. In the past, people were helped to cope with change because they had what Alvin Toffler calls 'personal stability zones'.[3] There were aspects of lives that did not change. Of these, the most important were a job for life, a marriage for life, and a place for life. Not everyone had them, but they were not rare. They gave people a sense of economic, personal and geographical continuity. They were the familiar that gave individuals strength to cope with the unfamiliar. Today these things are becoming ever harder to find. Almost no job in the global market is permanent. More and more employment is becoming part-time, short-term and contractual. Even businesses like the great Japanese companies or IBM, which used to pride themselves on their lifelong commitment to employees, are no longer able to do so in the rapidly changing environment of modern business. Marriage, the very matrix of continuity in traditional societies, is rapidly being eroded by serial relationships, cohabitation and divorce. Fewer people are marrying. Fewer marriages last a lifetime. In Britain, four in every ten children are born outside marriage. Four in every ten marriages end in divorce. The very concept of belonging to a place, a neighbourhood, a locality – somewhere we belong and call home – has all but disappeared. We travel and move, often because our work demands it. In the United States 20 per cent of people change homes every year. We face the maximum of uncertainty with the minimum of resources to protect us against insecurity. Change has become systemic. It no longer takes place within a frame of the things that do not change.

Most importantly, we no longer feel a sense of control over our lives. The great forces that surround us – financial markets, currency movements, technological change, the economic climate, the international arena, the natural environment – are becoming ever more volatile, complex and unpredictable. They no longer have identifiable agents. Instead they are the result of the uncoordinated responses of billions of individual decisions. Even governments in an age of powerful multinational corporations have highly circumscribed powers. If businesses do not like one country's economic or fiscal policy, they will move their production or financial base elsewhere. If individuals are frustrated by one government's ban on reproductive cloning or the purchase of organs for transplantation, they can travel to some other country where it is not yet prohibited. When nation-states become ever more limited in their ability to shape events, we begin to feel as if the car carrying us forward has no driver at the wheel.

Nor do we have any assurance that the complex processes that will shape our future have a natural tendency to equilibrium. In the late 1990s the economic crisis in South East Asia led to financial collapse in Russia and from there to Brazil. The Internet boom and subsequent slump were fuelled by computer-driven buying and selling patterns that exaggerated both upward and downward moves in share prices. Thomas Friedman devised a graphic phrase to describe the participants in the global market. He called them 'the electronic herd',[4] – and herds stampede. The leading metaphor of modernity was Newtonian physics with its stately choreography of predictable motion. Its counterparts in postmodernity are Heisenberg's uncertainty principle, chaos theory and reflexivity, all of which point to unpredictability and uncertain outcomes. One recent bestseller, Malcolm Gladwell's *The Tipping Point*, is dedicated to showing how changes in social trends, from fashion to crime, are best understood on the model of epidemiology, the process by which relatively isolated cases of a disease suddenly become an epidemic.[5] The more interconnected we become, through computer and modem networks, international travel and economic and environmental interdependence, the more likely it is that small disruptions will have large effects, partly by contagion, partly by the sheer mathematics of geometric progression, successive multiplications of change. None of this makes for comfort or security. 'Progress', wrote Robert Bellah, 'seems less compelling when it appears that it may be progress into the abyss.'[6]

A series of classic studies has analysed the connection between stress and control. In one, subjects were exposed to electric shocks of increasing intensity. Some were provided with a button by which they could stop the experiment; others were given none. Those who had the button were able to endure far higher levels of shock than the others.[7] Another study, this time of elderly people in residential homes, showed that when they were able to decide for themselves when visitors were to be admitted, choose their meals from a menu and decide what they were going to do that day, they felt healthier and actually lived longer than those whose decisions were taken for them by the staff.[8] Perceived lack of control is stress-inducing and debilitating. If that is our experience of many of the major dimensions of our lives, it too would explain the systemic anxiety that has become part of the twenty-first century mood.

*   *   *

I want, though, to take the analysis deeper into the subsoil of Western culture by looking at a central paradox in the leading concept of the market age: the idea of choice itself. Conflicting messages are being sent by the market on the one hand, and the life and social sciences on the other. Supermarkets, the Internet and e-commerce have multiplied choice beyond the experience of any previous generation. Whatever we want, we can effectively search the world within minutes and find it. I used to love going around second-hand bookshops to see if I could spot a title I had been looking for and was currently out of print. It might take me years to track down a particular volume, and often did. Today, thanks to on-line trading and the power of search engines, the same process takes seconds. I type in the name of the author and the title, and almost instantaneously I get back the results from several thousand book traders across the world. I miss the sense of adventure and serendipity, but the sheer convenience more than compensates for it. Markets maximize choice.

At the same time a whole series of quasi-scientific determinisms over the past four centuries have convinced us that choice is an illusion. Spinoza, Marx, Durkheim and Freud, each in their own way, undermined our image of man-the-choosing-animal. We are what we are, they argued, not because of what we have chosen to be, but because of social structure, economic forces, historical inevitability or early childhood conditioning. True freedom, said Spinoza, is consciousness of necessity. The ways in which we understand the world, argued Marx, are actually the result of a successful attempt by one class to maintain power over another.

Even quintessentially personal decisions like actual or attempted suicide, said Durkheim, are social phenomena and can be predicted without reference to individual intention. Beneath the surface of apparently rational behaviour, said Freud, lie buried memories and irrational instincts of which we are only dimly aware.

Perhaps nothing has done more to undermine the connection between character, choice and responsibility than the combined influences of Darwinism, evolutionary psychology and our advancing knowledge of the human genome. Our acts, argue the neo-Darwinians, are the result of instincts, which are to a large degree genetically encoded and emerged because of the spread of genes from one generation to the next. We take risks to protect our children, not because of the morality of parental responsibility and love, but because that is the way our genes get passed on across time. The combined result of these intellectual heritages is a comprehensive 'hermeneutics of suspicion'. Nothing is what it seems, least of all human behaviour. Courage, compassion, the noble deeds of heroic lives, are mere superstructures of illusion over a mindless and largely unconscious struggle for dominance and survival. As a result, at the very moment we are confronted with unprecedented choices, we have lost confidence in the salience of choice itself.

Even this understates the nature of our confusion. Something happens – a 'tipping point' is reached – when everything is open to choice and nothing, as it were, chooses us. One of the things that made the world intelligible to earlier generations was the *givenness* of much of life. Who you were, what your position in society was, who you married, what you did for a living, and much else depended on the accident of birth. Nor was this random. It was part of a total understanding of the universe. The structures of society, whether they were hierarchical, organic or divinely decreed, were one with the fabric of the cosmos. The individual was part of a pattern which had overall coherence and design. This gave identity a massive solidity, almost incomprehensible to us today.

There was much wrong with this worldview, and I for one have no desire to return to it. Much of modernity, that vast set of changes between the seventeenth and twentieth centuries, was a liberation of the individual from the social constraints of birth. Sociologists have a whole range of ways of describing it: from status to contract, *Gemeinschaft* to *Gesellschaft*, community to society, honour to dignity, and fate to choice.[9] The new economic and political order heralded by the market on the one hand, representative democracy on the other, represented a quantum leap for the individual and his or her ability to choose what to do, where to live, and how to construct a life. But no social process ends where one would like it to.

The 'individual' – that creation of the seventeenth century – had an identity, which is to say, a stable sense of self from birth to death. His or her life could be told as a narrative, factually in an autobiography, fictionally in a novel, both of them genres which achieved great popularity in the modern age. Something happens when change is so rapid that nothing confers meaning – when lives become lifestyles, commitments become experiments, relationships become provisional, careers turn into contracts, and life itself ceases to have the character of a narrative and becomes instead a series of episodes with no connecting thread. Jeremy Seabrook paints a graphic picture of a young woman, Michelle, from a Midlands council estate:

> At fifteen her hair was one day red, the next blond, then jet-black, then teased into Afro kinks and after that rat-tails, then plaited, and then cropped so that it glistened close to the skull ... Her lips were scarlet, then purple, then black. Her face was ghost-white and then peach-coloured, then bronze as if it were cast in metal. Pursued by dreams of flight, she left home at sixteen to be with her boyfriend, who was twenty-six ...
>
> At eighteen she returned to her mother, with two children ... She sat in the bedroom which she had fled three years earlier; the faded photos of yesterday's pop stars still stared down from the walls. She said she felt a hundred years old. She'd tried all that life could offer. Nothing else was left.[10]

This kind of existential burnout is a hazard of our times. Michelle is at the lower end of the economic spectrum, but a similar fate awaits her jet-setting counterpart in the upper echelons of the corporate world – flying from hotel to hotel, constantly in touch by mobile phone and handheld computer, watching financial markets around the world, always at risk of corporate downsizing, less and less in touch with those whose lives her decisions will affect, and guided by the brutal philosophy of the American bumper sticker that read, 'The guy with the most toys when he dies wins.'[11]

Advanced consumer cultures are built on a rapid succession of artificially induced and temporarily satisfied desires. When the market becomes not a mechanism of exchange but the guiding paradigm of life, then meaning itself is undermined. We turn, in Zygmunt Bauman's telling phrase, from 'pilgrims' to 'tourists'.[12] Society becomes ever less like a home, ever more like a hotel. We approach a state in which there is nowhere we belong, no one to whom we owe loyalty or who owes loyalty to us, no one with whom we share a destiny, no one for whom we hold lasting significance. Life becomes weightless, ever less connected to something solid and enduring beyond the self. Edmund Burke's famous words, more relevant now than they were when he wrote them in 1790, come to mind:

> By this unprincipled facility of changing the state as often, and as much, and in as many ways as there are floating fancies or fashions, the whole chain and continuity of the commonwealth would be broken. No one generation could link with the other. Men would become little better than the flies of a summer ... and thus the commonwealth itself would, in a few generations, crumble away, be disconnected into the dust and powder of individuality, and at length be dispersed to all the winds of heaven.[13]

Oscar Wilde defined a cynic as one who knows the price of everything but the value of nothing – reminding us that value inheres in those things (love, loyalty, altruism, faithfulness) that are not marketable; that are earned, not bought; part of who we are, not what we own. A culture in which everything can be bought is one that has devalued value and institutionalized cynicism.

Increasingly, what we buy are not only goods but personal services. This too has a narrowing effect on action by turning the things we once did personally or together into commodities we purchase for a price. In the course of the nineteenth and twentieth centuries much of this took place in the form of a transfer of responsibility – for education, welfare, health and law enforcement – from families and communities to the state. Today, it has moved beyond the state to the market. Vast swathes of personal relationship have been commodified and offered for sale in a seemingly endless proliferation of new services: counsellors, spiritual guides, personal trainers, style advisers, shopping consultants, massage therapists, aromatherapists, aerobics instructors, exercise class leaders – the whole spectrum of what Robert Reich calls 'paying for attention'.[14]

What once made relationships constitutive of personal identity and self-respect is precisely the fact that they stood *outside* the world of contracts and market exchange. Family, friends, neighbours, mentors, were people to whom you were bound by moral reciprocity. What was important is that they were there in bad times as well as good; when you needed them, not when you could pay for them. They told you things you didn't want to hear as well as the things you did. Compare that to the marketization of friendship in the form of the advertisement for a 'personal coach' quoted by Robert Reich: 'Best friends are wonderful to have. But is your best friend a professional who you will trust to work with you on the most important aspects of your life?' The answer to this rhetorical question is Yes: you *trust* a friend precisely because you do *not* pay for his or her friendship.

The ever increasing demands of work mean that people have less time to spend on relationships – children, parents, friends, fellow members of a congregation, co-workers in voluntary and philanthropic groups – which further narrows and fragments our sense of self, as well as creating new social divides between those who can and those who can't 'pay for attention'. It is worth recalling that it was none other than Adam Smith who wrote that the 'disposition to admire, and almost to worship, the rich and the powerful, and to despise, or at least, to neglect, persons of poor and mean condition' is 'the great and most universal cause of the corruption of our moral sentiments'.[15]

We have delegated away much of what matters in our lives, partly to governments, police forces, judges, courts, social workers, managers and teachers, in part to therapists, counsellors, advisers, coaches and gurus, each of whom we pay, through taxation or fees, to manage our affairs, relationships, conflicts or emotions better than we can or have time to do. This constitutes a massive loss of sovereignty over our lives, and it means that when things go wrong, as at times they must, we are liable to despair, because our destiny now rests in other hands, not our own. That is the weakness of contracting out large aspects of our lives, as against assuming personal and moral responsibility.

* * *

The word 'moral' is crucial here. Morality has had a hard time of it in the past half-century. It has come to represent everything we believe ourselves to have been liberated from: authority, repression, the delay of instinctual gratification, all that went with the religious, puritanical, Victorian culture of our grand-parents. Virtues once thought admirable – modesty, humility, discretion, restraint – are now dusty exhibits in a museum of the cultural curiosities. Words like 'duty', 'obligation', 'judgement', 'wisdom' either carry a negative charge or no meaning at all. What I have never seen clearly stated is the simple fact that systems of morality were (not always, but sometimes) an attempt to *fight despair in the name of hope*, and recover human dignity by reinstating us as subjects not objects, the authors of our deeds and of our lives.

It is no accident that the word 'demoralization' has a double sense.[16] It signals both a loss of moral meanings and a loss of hope. We are made most anxious by things outside our control. Ancient civilizations were dominated by fears of natural catastrophe –

drought, floods, famine – and much of their creative energy went into personifying these forces as gods who might be placated by incantation, ritual or magic. Today we are no less fearful of vast forces – technology, the erosion of the biosphere, the globalization of industry, the internationalization of terror – but we have no story or myth through which to personalize them, rendering them intelligible and capable of being influenced by what we do. Our hopes are invested in governments, from which we demand more and expect less, or in markets which by their nature are capricious and indifferent to those they benefit and those they harm. At the core of our culture is the knowledge that too much of what happens to us is beyond our control, the result of economic choices or political decisions taken far away by people we will never meet nor be able to identify. Beyond the narrowing circle of the self lies a world in which we are not the makers but the made. This is the genesis of despair.

Against just such a backdrop, some 4,000 years ago, there emerged a different conception of human life. It suggested that individuals are not powerless in the face of the impersonal. We can create families, communities, even societies, around the ideals of love and fellowship and trust. In such societies, individuals are valued not for what they own or the power they wield but for what they are. They are not immune to conflict or tragedy, but when these strike, the individual is not alone. He or she is surrounded by networks of support, extended families, friends and neighbours. These relationships do not simply happen. Much of the energy of communities such as these is dedicated to ensuring that they happen, through education, social sanction and careful protection of human institutions. Children are habituated into virtues and rules of conduct. They learn to value the 'We' as well as the 'I'. The rewards of a moral order are great. It creates an island of interpersonal meaning in a sea of impersonal forces. It redeems individuals from solitude. Morality is civilization's greatest attempt to humanize fate.

The power of this vision is that it locates the source of action within ourselves. It restores the dignity of agency and responsibility. It leads us to see our lives not as the blind play of external causes – the genome, the free market, economic interests, social forces and advertising-induced fashions – but as a series of choices in pursuit of the right and good, choices in which we are not left unguided but for which a vast store of historical experience lies at our disposal. It reminds us that the acts we perform, the decisions we take, make a difference: to our family, to our friends and associates, to our sense of a life well lived. It teaches us to cherish and sustain the relationships – marriage, families, friendships, communities – which give us strength as we face the uncertainties of an open future. It removes the randomness of a life lived in border skirmishes between our desires and those of others. It allows us to see ourselves as on a journey, begun by those who came before us and whose histories we share, to be continued by those who come after us of whose hopes we are the guardians, a journey towards a remote but intelligible destination, the good society we are called on to create together.

The deepest insight I received into what makes a life worth living was not at university but when I began my career as a rabbi and had, for the first time, to officiate at funerals. They were distressing moments, trying to comfort a family in the midst of grief, and I never found them easy, but they were extraordinarily instructive. In my address I had to paint a portrait of the deceased, whom I might not have known personally, so I would talk first to the family and friends to try to understand what he or she meant to them. Almost always they spoke of similar things. The person who had died had been a supportive marriage partner, a caring parent. He or she had been a loyal friend, ready to help when help was needed. No one ever mentioned what they earned or bought, what car they drove, where they spent their holidays. The people most mourned were not the most rich or successful. They were people who enhanced the lives of others. They were kind. You could rely on them. They had a sense of responsibility. They gave time as well as money to voluntary causes. They were part of a community, living its values, sharing its griefs and celebrations. As this pattern repeated itself time and again, I realized that I was learning about more than the deceased. I was being educated into what makes a life well lived.

It had little if anything to do with the values of a market society and everything to do with moral principle – good deeds, caring relationships, a willingness to make sacrifices for values one did not construct oneself, belonging to a community dedicated to the pursuit of ideals. These are the values that give continuity and dignity to a life. They are a large part of what most of us understand by happiness. They are curiously egalitarian. They are about what we do and are, not about power or wealth, success or prestige. They are strikingly at odds with the assumptions of a consumer society on the one hand, scientific determinism on the other.

Morality is integral to the ecology of hope because it locates social change at a level at which we can make a difference through the acts we do, the principles by which we live, and the relationships we create. It sees us as something other than replaceable parts of an economic system; it grants us a form of independence from the whims and passing interests of others. Within a moral community, marriage gives permanence to love. Loyalty gives strength to parenthood. Education becomes a conversation between the generations. Kinship and covenant link us to our fellow human beings so that they know they can rely on us and we know we can rely on them. The knowledge that we are strangers teaches us to reach beyond the boundary of 'us' and extend friendship and reciprocity to 'them'. The knowledge, too, that the earth is not ours, that we are temporary residents, heirs of those who came before us and guardians for those who will come after us in turn, steers us away from the destructive impulse – whether to war or premature genetic intervention or excessive exploitation – which may sometimes come to those who have no stake in a future beyond their lifetime.

* * *

It may well be that religious communities are one of the few environments in which these values are still sustained. Certainly Durkheim, a century ago, argued that this was one of their primary functions: to embody collective judgements on the good, the morally valuable, the holy. This itself may be a reason why, in large parts of the world, religion has had such a revival. The idea that happiness is to be found in getting and spending, the fiction sustained by advanced economies, has never been seriously entertained by any thinker, religious or philosophical, who has pondered the question. Wealth, fame, success – these things are too randomly distributed, too external to who we are, too loosely related to merit, worth or desert, to provide a meaningful framework for a life. A minimal requirement of a gracious social order is that it provides equal access to the sources of self-respect, and this must therefore be something less vulnerable to chance than one's place in an economic system.

The power of the great religions is that they do more than offer a vision of the good. That could be equally said of philosophical systems. Unlike philosophical systems, however, they embody it in the life of a community. They make it vivid and substantial in prayer and ritual, in compelling narratives and collective acts of rededication. I do not wish to argue that religions individually or collectively are our sole source of morality. That is manifestly untrue. They remain, however, a significant space outside of and in counterpoint to a late-modern Western culture that tends systematically to dissolve the values and virtues that give meaning to a life. That may be why they have become, in countries outside the West – and to a noticeable degree within the West itself – a cogent form of protest against its values.

It is just here, however, that we have to take seriously the disciplines and constraints of the dignity of difference. Religions do not agree with one another, nor with secular philosophies, when it comes to some of the great moral issues: abortion, euthanasia, *in vitro* fertilization, stem-cell research, homosexuality, cohabitation outside marriage and many other divisive matters. It is this very potential for bitter conflict that leads people to embrace moral relativism on the one hand (if religions do not agree, then morality is mere choice), libertarianism on the other (society should pass no collective judgement on moral matters; morality is a private affair). Both of these positions are, I believe, false. We argue about morality in a way, and with a seriousness, we do not about matters that really are relative (how to dress for a dinner party, for example). And we do not truly believe that moral issues are private – if we did, there would be no protests on environmental or human rights issues, no public moral debate at all. Yet the question is real and urgent: how do we live with moral difference and yet sustain an overarching community?

The answer, I have already suggested, is *conversation* – not mere debate but the disciplined act of communicating (making my views intelligible to someone who does not share them) and listening (entering into the inner world of someone whose views are opposed to my own). Each is a genuine form of respect, of paying attention to the other, of conferring value on his or her opinions even though they are not mine. In a debate one side wins, the other loses, but both are the same as they were before. In a conversation neither side loses and both are changed, because they now know what reality looks like from a different perspective. That is not to say that either gives up its previous convictions. That is not what conversation is about. It does mean, however, that I may now realize that I must make space for another deeply held belief, and if my own case has been compelling, the other side may understand that it too must make space for mine. That is how public morality is constructed in a plural society – not by a single dominant voice, nor by the relegation of moral issues to the private domain of home and local congregation, but by a sustained act of understanding and seeking to be understood across the boundaries of difference.

In a plural society – all the more so in a plural world – each of us has to settle for less than we do when we associate with fellow believers. A Catholic may believe that abortion is murder, a Jew or Muslim that sex outside marriage is forbidden, and these convictions are given life within our respective communities of faith. But we cannot seek to have them imposed by force of law on those who are not members of our community if there are other groups who seriously disagree and make a compelling case for the right to construct a life along different lines. Yet what we lose is more than compensated for by the fact that together we are co-architects of a society larger than we could construct on our own, one in which our voice is heard and attended to even if it does not carry the day. Just as community is built on the willingness to let the 'I' be shaped by the 'We', so society is made by the readiness to let the 'We' of our community be constrained by the need to make space for other communities and their deeply held beliefs. Society is a conversation scored for many voices. But it is precisely in and through that conversation that we become conjoint authors of our collective future, rather than dust blown by the wind of economic forces. Conversation – respectful, engaged, reciprocal, calling forth some of our greatest powers of empathy and understanding – is the moral form of a world governed by the dignity of difference.

*   *   *

There is no way of eliminating the objective conditions that create insecurity. We are entering on a century whose trajectory is radically unpredictable, and the very freedoms we value make it so. I have, however, argued in this chapter that we have intellectual resources that enable us to cope with it. Of these the most important is a moral vision. That is what the nineteenth century had and we so often lack. It was what enabled Abraham Lincoln to heal the wounds left by civil war ('With malice toward none, with charity for all'), and Disraeli to invest political change with ethical drama ('justice is truth in action'). When used today – most notably by Nelson Mandela in invoking ideas of truth and reconciliation to heal the wounds of apartheid – it still retains its pristine power. We need such a moral template. We can travel at speed so long as we know where we are going. It is when we lose a sense of vision that we find ourselves, in effect, without a map or a destination. That is when people turn to populist leaders capable of manipulating public fear, or to regressive identities and fundamentalisms that allow them to cope with fear by blaming some group or other for being the cause of the world's ills. These are possibilities I never thought I would have to warn against in my lifetime, so great were the catastrophes they brought about in the twentieth century. But when feelings run high, memories are short.

What morality restores to an increasingly uncertain world is the idea of *responsibility* – that what we do, severally and collectively, makes a difference, and that the future lies in our hands. Every era has produced its own philosophies, or quasi-scientific systems to show that what happens could not have been otherwise; that the march of history is inevitable; that it is hubris to believe we can fight against fate. All we can do is to align ourselves to its flow, exploit it when we can, and render ourselves stoically indifferent to our fate when we cannot. That is the kind of argument all too often made for globalization. It exists; it is inescapable; it is an elemental force; it is what Thomas Friedman calls the 'golden straitjacket'.[17] There is no choice but to join and prosper or stand aloof and starve. This way of thinking is a regression to a view of the universe that is very ancient indeed. It is the world of myth, in which mankind is alone in an environment dominated by irresistible forces blind to our presence, deaf to our prayers and hopes.

The great leap of the biblical imagination was to argue otherwise. There is a personal dimension to existence. Our hopes are not mere dreams, nor are our ideals illusions. Something at the core of being responds to us as persons, inviting us to exercise our freedom by shaping families, communities and societies in such a way as to honour the image of God that is mankind, investing each human life with ultimate dignity. This view, shared by Judaism, Christianity and Islam, sees choice, agency and moral responsibility at the heart of the human project. We are not powerless in the face of fate. Every technological advance can be used for good or evil. Every economic order can be exploited, allowed to run free, or directed by considerations of justice and equity. There is nothing inevitably benign or malign in our increasing powers. It depends on the use we make of them. What we can create, we can control. What we initiate, we can direct. With every new power come choice, responsibility and exercise of the moral imagination. I believe that this view – always opposed by determinisms ancient and modern – is not merely true but necessary if we are to defeat the politics of insecurity and fear.

Global capitalism is not a juggernaut that no one can steer. It arose in unplanned, unexpected ways, but it does not have to stay that way. The environmental movement in the 1970s changed public opinion and patterns of consumption. The anti-globalization protests of the late 1990s made governments and international financial institutions think again about their responsibilities to the developing world. Campaigns against corporations have led them to take greater care that their goods are not produced under unacceptable working conditions for starvation wages. All of us, by the decisions we make about how we live and work and travel and consume help to shape an environment. To think and act morally, to do what is right because it is right, influences others; it begins to create a climate of opinion; good, like evil, is infectious. We do not have to accept the unacceptable. The only thing that makes social or economic trends inevitable is the belief that they are. The unfolding drama of the twenty-first century is one of which we are the co-writers of the script. It can be turned this way or that by collective consent. Our aim must be to settle for nothing else than an economic system that maximizes human dignity. We must hand on to future generations a more gracious, less capricious and inequitable world.

NOTES

1. Wright 2000, p. 50.
2. Ogburn 1964.
3. Toffler 1971, p. 341.
4. Friedman 2000, p. 112.
5. Gladwell 2001.
6. Bellah et al. 1988, p. 277.
7. Geer, et al. 1970.
8. Langer and Rodin 1976.
9. See, for example, Berger et al. 1973.
10. Quoted in Bauman 1998, p. 91.
11. Demos 1998, p. 3.
12. Bauman 1998, pp. 77–102.
13. Burke 1993, pp. 95–6.
14. Reich (2001), pp. 172–89.
15. Smith (1976), p. 126.
16. Here I draw from Sacks (2000).
17. Friedman (2000), pp. 101–11.

Chapter 5

Contribution: The Moral Case for the Market Economy

Mankind's livelihood requires his active participation. Apart from the period of [the Israelites'] wandering in the wilderness, and other times of miraculous intervention, there is no manna from heaven. This active participation of man in the creation of his own wealth is a sign of spiritual greatness. In this respect we are, as it were, imitators of God.

(Rabbenu Bachya)

Mankind was not created to serve markets. Markets were made to serve mankind. In the previous chapter I noted that advocates of globalization are often guilty of the argument from inevitability. The free market, they say, is here to stay whether we like it or not. Communism and socialism were tried and failed. All those who wish to create higher living standards must embrace globalization and its disciplines. There is no other way than to put on 'the golden straitjacket'.[1]

There is much to be said for the new economy. Deregulated markets, the massive international flow of investment funds and new information-based technologies have increased prosperity, not only for individuals but for 'the wealth of nations'. But every system has limits. The market is good at creating wealth but not at distributing it. It encourages certain virtues but undermines others. It has social consequences that are not always benign and sometimes disastrous. Markets are the best way we know of structuring exchanges – goods to be bought or sold. They are far from the best way of ordering relationships or preserving goods whose value is not identical with their price. Inevitably, societies face choices that cannot be resolved by economics alone. The argument from inevitability is a way of sidestepping the moral issues any institution must face, especially one as intimately related to the conditions of life on earth as is the global economy. I have argued that we may not abdicate responsibility for the world we hand on to our children. One of the forms this abdication takes is what George Soros calls 'market fundamentalism'[2]– the idea that we can leave it to the market to take care of its own consequences. We cannot. That rests with us, severally and collectively, as global citizens. What I want to do in this and the following chapters is to explore the moral dimensions of the market in a global age – the values that should guide us if we are to create a more humane world.

If anything has a moral dimension, economics does. According to the fourth-century Talmudic teacher Rava, when we leave this life and enter the world to come, the first question we will be asked is: 'Did you deal honestly in business?'[3] Only subsequently will we be asked about other aspects of our lives. In the school of Rabbi Ishmael (second century) it was taught that whoever conducts himself with integrity in his economic affairs is as if he fulfilled the whole of the religious life.[4] The Talmud suggests that one who wishes to achieve sainthood should occupy himself in study and practice of the ethical laws relating to commerce and finance.[5] At one of the critical points in the Jewish calendar, on the Sabbath before the Ninth of Av, the day of mourning for the destruction of the Temple, we read in the synagogue the great first chapter of Isaiah with its insistence that without political and economic virtue, religious piety is vain:

Seek justice, encourage the oppressed,
Defend the cause of the fatherless,
Plead the case of the widow ...
Your silver has become dross,

Your choice wine is diluted with water,
Your rulers are rebels, companions of thieves;
They all love bribes and chase after gifts. (Isaiah 1: 17–23)

The perennial temptations of the market – to pursue gain at someone else's expense, to take advantage of ignorance, to treat employees with indifference – needed to be fought against. Canons of fair trading and conditions of employment have to be established and policed. From a Jewish perspective this is part of the religious life, because the relationship between man and God cannot be divorced from that between man and man. Morality belongs no less in the boardroom than in the bedroom, in the market-place as much as in a house of prayer.

Of any economic system we must ask: Does it enhance human dignity? Does it create self-respect? Does it encourage creativity? Does it allow everyone to participate in the material blessings of this created world? Does it sustain a climate of equal regard – for employees as well as employers, the poor no less than the rich? Does it protect the vulnerable and help those in need to escape the trap of need? Does it ensure that no one lacks the means for a dignified existence? Do those who succeed share their blessings with those who have less? Does the economic system strengthen the bonds of human solidarity? And does it know its own limits – does it recognize that its values are not the only values, that there is more to life than a perpetual striving after wealth, that the market is not the only mechanism of distribution, and that an economic system is a means not an end?

These are the questions we must ask of global capitalism if we are to exercise responsibility. The ethical imperative is ubiquitous and non-negotiable. Beyond every 'is' lies the claim of 'ought'. No system – not scientific or political or economic – is self-justifying, worthy of endorsement just because it happens to be what it is. That is what I want to explore in this and the next four chapters, beginning with the market itself and the values it embodies and to which it gives rise.

* * *

We owe to Max Weber the insight that economic orders are influenced by religious ones. His view, famously, is that the 'spirit of capitalism' owed its existence to 'the Protestant ethic', Calvinism especially.[6] More recently, Michael Novak has written about the affinity between the Catholic ethic and capitalism.[7] The contribution of Islam to the development of finance and trade is significant and goes back as far as the eighth century, when Baghdad and Basra became world centres of commerce. The vast extent of the Islamic empire encouraged trust and trade between distant lands, and the Hanafite school of Islamic jurisprudence, in particular, pioneered in the development of business contracts.[8] So there is no specifically Jewish association with the market economy. Undeniably, though, Jews did play an important part in its development. As Werner Sombart pointed out:

> [T]he importance of the Jews was twofold. On the one hand, they influenced the outward form of modern capitalism; on the other, they gave expression to its inward spirit. Under the first heading, the Jews contributed no small share in giving to economic relations the international aspect they bear today; in helping the modern state, that framework of capitalism, to become what it is; and lastly in giving the capitalist organization its peculiar features, by inventing a good many details of the commercial machinery which moves the business life of today, and by co-operating in the perfecting of others. Under the second heading, the importance of the Jews is so enormous because they, above all others, endowed economic life with its modern spirit . . .[9]

To be sure, no religion can be identified with a single economic order. There were communists of Jewish ancestry and inspiration – Karl Marx, Rosa Luxemburg and Leon Trotsky among them – and there were many Jewish socialist groups in the early twentieth century, the Eastern European Bund being the most influential. In Second Temple times, the Essenes lived in property-sharing communes, an experiment revived in modern Israel in the form of the kibbutz system.[10] Ethical socialism draws much of its inspiration from the exodus narrative and the prophets of ancient Israel.[11] None the less, Judaism has tended to favour the free market, while subjecting it to criticism in the light of its ideals.

This was, once, a countercultural stance. We tend to forget how recent and relatively unforeseen was the victory of the market economy over its rivals: communism, socialism and older, more hierarchical regimes. Set against it was a long intellectual history of disdain for trade. Plato, in *The Republic*, argued that shopkeepers are 'generally men not strong enough to be of use in any other occupation' and consigned them to the third and lowest class of society.[12] Aristotle, in *The Politics*, called the life of commerce 'ignoble and inimical to excellence'.[13] Military societies saw business as an unmanly enterprise. No less a figure than Adam Smith said that a commercial culture 'sinks the courage of mankind, and tends to extinguish martial spirit'.[14] Religious thinkers denigrated it as materialism. Aquinas, conceding that business need not be 'sinful or contrary to virtue', none the less insisted that priests should not take part in it because it would divert them from matters of the spirit.[15] More collectivist thinkers contrasted altruism with the competitiveness and 'possessive individualism' of the market. J. A. Hobson, for example, argued that 'By their very nature the bargaining processes inhibit the consideration of the good of others, and concentrate the mind and will of each party upon the bargaining for his own immediate and material gains ... This constant drive of selfish interests involves a hardening of the moral arteries.'[16] It is important, therefore to understand why Judaism, *on ethical and spiritual grounds*, favoured the market economy.

* * *

In his masterly survey, *The Wealth and Poverty of Nations*, David Landes sets out to understand why some economies grow while others remain stagnant.[17] One of the questions he raises, for example, is why the industrial revolution took place in Europe, not China. In the Middle Ages, China was far in advance of the West. It was the first country to witness the invention of printing, paper, porcelain and explosives. Why then was it Europe that leapt ahead in the nineteenth century? Landes' answer has been challenged by some scholars, but it is broadly this: that *culture*, not natural resources, climate or other material factors, makes the difference. Europe had what China did not: a Judeo-Christian ethic.

Landes identifies several significant features of this ethic. First is the biblical respect for property rights. This he sees as nothing less than a revolution against the ancient world and the power it gave rulers to regard the property of the tribe or the people as their own. By contrast, when Moses finds his leadership challenged by the Israelites during the Korach rebellion, he says about his relation to the people, 'I have not taken one ass from them nor have I wronged any one of them' (Numbers 16: 15). For a ruler to abuse property rights is, for the Hebrew Bible, one of the great corruptions of power. Judaism is the religion of a people born in slavery and longing for redemption. The great assault of slavery against human dignity is that it deprives me of the ownership of the wealth I create.

Perhaps the most influential single phrase in Western civilization is the verse in the first chapter of Genesis in which God says, 'Let us make man in Our image and likeness' (1: 26). What is revolutionary in these words is not that a human being can be in the image of God. That was an idea familiar to the ancient world. Sumerian kings and Egyptian Pharaohs were precisely that: gods, or representatives of the gods, in human form. What was new was not that *a* human being can be in the image of God, but that *every* human being is. From its inception, Judaism was a living protest against hierarchical societies that give some, but not all, dignity, power and freedom. Instead it insisted that if any individual is sacred, then every individual is, because each of us is in the image of God.

The central question therefore is: how do we build social structures that honour and sustain the freedom, integrity and creativity of the individual? The brief answer is that the Hebrew Bible is an extended critique of what we would today call big government. At one extreme is the biblical portrait of ancient Egypt, a nation which builds extraordinary buildings but at the cost of turning human beings into slaves. At the opposite extreme we have the justly famous eighth chapter of I Samuel, in which the people come to the prophet and demand a king. On the instruction of God, Samuel tells them that if they appoint a king, he will eventually seize their sons and daughters, fields and vineyards, and a percentage of their harvests and cattle. Even constitutional monarchy, in other words, will involve a sacrifice of rights of property and person. 'When that day comes, you will cry out for relief from the king you have chosen, and the Lord will not answer you on that day' (I Samuel 8: 18).

The classic Judaic view is that governments are necessary for defence and the maintenance of social order. As a rabbinic teaching of the first century CE puts it: 'Pray for the welfare of the government, for were it not for the fear of it, people would eat one another alive.'[18] But state action always stands in need of justification, because any government, however democratically elected, *ipso facto* represents a curtailment of certain fundamental rights such as the right to enjoy the fruits of one's own labour. It can only be justified on the grounds that secure possession of those rights depends on the existence of a central power that defends individuals against lawlessness on the one hand, and foreign invasion on the other. Long before Hobbes, Locke and Jefferson, therefore, biblical Judaism is a theory of *limited government*. This principled insistence on the moral limits of power is the only secure defence of the individual against the collective, whether it be the tyranny of kings or what John Stuart Mill, following Alexis de Tocqueville, called the 'tyranny of the majority'. God, in the Hebrew Bible, seeks the free worship of free human beings, and two of the most powerful defences of freedom are private property and economic independence.

* * *

A second factor Landes identifies in the Judeo-Christian tradition is the biblical respect for the inherent dignity of labour. God tells Noah that he will be saved from the flood, but it is Noah who has to build the ark. The high value Judaism sets on work is well brought out in the following passage:

> Rabbi Shimon ben Elazar said: Great is work because even Adam did not taste food until he had performed work, as it is said, 'The Lord God took the man and placed him in the Garden of Eden to till it and preserve it' (Genesis 2: 15). Only then do we read, 'The Lord God commanded the man: From every tree of the garden you may eat' (Genesis 2: 16).[19]

This is a subtle observation. A superficial reading of Genesis can convey the impression that work is not a blessing but a curse, for it was only when he was exiled from paradise that man was told that his fate would be toil: 'By the sweat of your brow you will eat your food.' Not so, says Rabbi Shimon. In Eden itself, Adam was told to till the earth. Though food lay all around him, he had to labour first.

Work, though not itself a religious act, is a condition of human dignity. 'Six days shall you labour and do all your work, but the seventh day is a Sabbath to the Lord your God' – meaning that we serve God through work as well as rest. The Jewish liturgy for Saturday night – the point at which the day of rest ends – culminates in a hymn to the values of work: 'When you eat of the labour of your hands, you are happy and it shall be well with you.' On this, the rabbis commented, 'You are happy' refers to this life; 'It shall be well with you' refers to life in the world to come.[20] Work, in other words, has *spiritual* value, because earning our food is part of the stature, the creativity of the human condition:

> When the Holy One, blessed be He, told Adam, 'The ground will be cursed because of you ... it will bring forth thorns and thistles,' Adam wept. He said, 'Lord of the Universe, am I and my ass to eat in the same manger?' But when he heard the words 'By the sweat of your brow you will eat bread,' he was consoled.[21]

Labour elevates man, for by it he *earns* his food. What concerned the rabbis was the self-respect that came from work as against unearned income. To eat without working was not a boon but an escape from the human situation. Animals *find* sustenance; only mankind *creates* it. As the thirteenth-century commentator Rabbenu Bachya put it, 'The active participation of man in the creation of his own wealth is a sign of his spiritual greatness.'[22] Jewish law invalidates gamblers from serving as witnesses since they are not members of the productive economy. They do not 'contribute to the settlement of the world'.[23]

This is in marked contrast to the ethics of ancient Greece. Plutarch, for example, says that we may be pleased with a piece of work while still regarding those who produced it as 'low and sordid people'. In Plato's *Gorgias*, Socrates asks Callicles whether he would permit his daughter to marry the son of an engineer. Aristotle concedes that a society needs agricultural workers and craftsmen, but their work is for serfs and slaves, not free citizens of the *polis*. In Greek myth the gods did not work, unlike Genesis in which our first view of God is of a craftsman fashioning a universe.[24] Judaism never developed an aristocratic or cloistered ethic, dismissive of the productive economy. The great rabbis were themselves labourers, businessmen or professionals. They knew that the Jewish community needed an economic as well as a spiritual base. Accordingly, the Talmud lists as one of the duties of a parent, to teach one's child a craft or trade through which he can earn a living.[25]

The greatest of medieval rabbis, Moses Maimonides, fought against the practice of supporting a leisured class of rabbinic scholars through public charitable funds. 'One who makes his mind up to study Torah and not to work but to live on charity', he wrote, 'profanes the name of God, brings the Torah into contempt, extinguishes the light of religion, brings evil upon himself, and deprives himself of life hereafter.'[26] This was a controversial campaign, never entirely successful, for in Judaism study is the highest value, and there were always those who believed that there should be a scholarly elite relieved of the burden of having to work for a living. Maimonides, though, saw the dangers of such an arrangement. It compromised the independence of the scholar. 'Better', he told his disciple Joseph ibn Aknin, 'to earn a penny as a tailor, carpenter or weaver than to depend on the income of the Exilarch.'[27] It removed the rabbi from the world in which his disciples had to live. And it turned a religious vocation into a paid profession.

Work achieves two things. First it gives a person *independence*, one of the essentials of a free society. The Jewish grace after meals contains a striking phrase: 'Please, God, do not make us dependent on the gifts of men.' Though Judaism places a high value on philanthropy, it values economic independence more. Any employment is better than none. 'Flay carcasses in the market-place', said the third-century teacher Rav, 'and do not say: I am a priest and a great man and it is beneath my dignity.'[28] The rabbis would have agreed with David Hume when he wrote, 'Nothing tends so much to corrupt and enervate and debase the mind as dependency, and nothing gives such noble and generous notions of probity as freedom and independency.'

The second, no less significant, is *creativity*. The biblical story of mankind begins with the command, 'Be fruitful and multiply, fill the earth and subdue it.' Work is more than mere labour. Biblical Hebrew has two words to express the difference: *melakhah* is work as creation, *avodah* is work as service or servitude. *Melakhah* is the arena in which we transform the world and thus become, in the striking rabbinic phrase, 'partners with God in the work of creation'.[29] God, taught Rabbi Akiva in the second century, deliberately left the world unfinished so that it could be completed by the work of human beings.[30] The creative God seeks creativity from mankind. That too is one of the advantages of free trade – the premium it places on constant innovation. As Le Mercier de la Rivière put it in the eighteenth century:

> The personal interest which this great freedom encourages, strongly and continually urges every individual to improve, to multiply the things that he wishes to sell; in this way to enlarge the mass of enjoyments which he can provide for other men, in order to enlarge by this means, the enjoyments that other men can provide for him in exchange. Thus the world goes by itself; the desire for enjoyment and the

freedom to enjoy, never ceasing to induce the multiplication of products and the growth of industry, impress on the whole of the society a motion which becomes a perpetual tendency towards its best possible condition.[31]

Max Weber argued that one of the revolutions of biblical thought was to demythologize, or disenchant, nature. For the first time human beings could see the condition of the world not as something sacrosanct and wrapped in mystery, but as something that could be rationally understood and improved upon.[32] This perspective, central to Judaism, makes it surprisingly open to new technologies, whether medical in the form of genetic engineering, stem-cell research and therapeutic cloning, or educational, in the form of the Internet and interactive CD-ROMs.

* * *

Most significant of all, perhaps, was Judaism's candid view of wealth as God's blessing, to be enjoyed as such. The world is God's creation; therefore it is good, and prosperity is a sign of God's blessing. Asceticism and self-denial have little place in Jewish spirituality. Rav, the third-century sage, went so far as to say: 'In the world to come we will face judgement for every legitimate pleasure we denied ourselves in this life.'[33] One of the recurring themes of the Book of Deuteronomy is 'You shall rejoice in all the good things the Lord your God has given to you and your household.'[34]

The economic growth produced by globalization and information technology has *religious* significance first and foremost because of the degree to which, more than any previous economic order, it allows us to alleviate poverty. Throughout its history, Judaism resisted any attempt to romanticize, rationalize or anaesthetize the pain of hunger, starvation or need. They would utterly have rejected Marx's description of religion as the opium of the people. Poverty is not a blessed or divinely ordained condition. It is, the rabbis said, 'a kind of death' and 'worse than 50 plagues'. They added:

Nothing is harder to bear than poverty, because he who is crushed by poverty is like one to whom all the troubles of the world cling and upon whom all the curses of Deuteronomy have descended. If all other troubles were placed one side and poverty on the other, poverty would outweigh them all.[35]

Nor did they take a high-minded view of the motives that lay behind wealth-creation. The great advocates of the market, Bernard Mandeville, David Hume and Adam Smith, were struck by something that many considered to be scandalous, namely that the market produces its collective benefits through a series of actions and transactions that are essentially self-regarding. As Adam Smith put it: 'It is not from the benevolence of the butcher, the brewer, or the baker, that we expect our dinner, but from their regard to their own interest.'[36] Within the market economy, in Smith's famous words, the individual 'intends only his own gain, and he is, in this, as in many other cases, led by an invisible hand to promote an end which was no part of his intention'.[37] This fact, that markets work on the basis of self-interest rather than altruism, has long led to criticism of everything suggested by the word 'commercial'.

Not so within Judaism, which accepted that the greatest advances are sometimes brought about through worldly and not necessarily high-minded motives. 'I saw', says Ecclesiastes, 'that all labour and all achievement spring from man's envy of his neighbour' (4: 4). Or, as the Talmudic sages put it, 'Were it not for the evil inclination, no one would build a house, marry a wife, have children, or engage in business.'[38] Purity of heart is essential to the relationship between man and God. But in relations between man and man, what matters is the outcome, not the sentiment which brought it about. From this perspective, Sir James Frazer was right when he said that 'it is better for the world that men should be right from wrong motives than that they would do wrong with the best intentions'.

What concerned the sages was the elimination of poverty, less through redistributive taxation than by creating a society in which the poor had access to help when they needed it, through charity to be sure, but also and especially through job creation. Hence with wealth came responsibility. *Richesse oblige.* Successful businessmen and women (the famous 31st chapter of Proverbs, 'A woman of strength who can find?' is essentially a hymn of praise to the businesswoman) were expected to set an example of public generosity and communal leadership. Conspicuous consumption was frowned upon, and periodically banned through local 'sumptuary laws'. Since wealth was a divine blessing, it carried with it an obligation to use it for the benefit of the community as a whole.

What is therefore morally unacceptable about the new economy from a Jewish point of view is not the free market itself, but the breakdown it is creating in the sense of social solidarity, the increasing segregation of the wealthy from the poor, and the waning sense of the responsibilities of success – what J. K. Galbraith called 'the culture of contentment'.[39] As corporations and their high-flyers are free to relocate, their contribution to the tax burden – and thus to collective provision of education, health and welfare – has steadily declined. The new class – the 'symbolic analysts' – is less engaged with the disadvantaged, less likely to meet and mix with them, and less inclined to use public services, than were their predecessors. That is wrong. It turns poverty into social exclusion and threatens to make it a fate passed on across the generations. It means that wealth, instead of strengthening community, weakens it.

The rabbis favoured markets and competition because they generated wealth, lowered prices, increased choice, reduced absolute levels of poverty, and in the course of time extended humanity's control over the environment, narrowing the extent to which we are the passive victims of circumstance and fate. Competition releases energy and creativity, but it must also serve the general good. So Jewish law permitted protectionist policies when they were essential to safeguard the local economy, especially when the outside trader did not pay taxes. There were also times when the rabbis intervened to lower prices of essential commodities. Provided, therefore, that the free market went hand in hand with strong communities and their attendant responsibilities, they welcomed its positive features, nowhere more so than in their own professional sphere of Jewish education. An established teacher could not object to a rival setting up in competition. The reason they gave for this ruling illustrates their general approach. They said simply, 'Jealousy among scholars increases wisdom.'[40]

Perhaps the best summary of Jewish economic ethics was given by the Catholic writer Michael Novak:

> In both its prophetic and rabbinic traditions Jewish thought has always felt comfortable with a certain well-ordered worldliness, whereas the Christian has always felt a pull toward otherworldliness. Jewish thought has had a candid orientation toward private property, commercial activity, markets, and profits, whereas Catholic thought – articulated from an early period chiefly among priests and monks – has persistently tried to direct the attention of its adherents beyond the activities and interests of this world to the next.[41]

* * *

Thus far, I have spoken about the Jewish approach to the market economy. It exists not because it is inevitable but because it is the best system yet devised for raising living standards and ensuring the independence and human dignity on which a free society depend. Whether it distributes wealth as successfully as it creates it is a question to which I turn in the next chapter. But there is one more argument to be made, and it is central to the theme of this book. The very act of market exchange is the supreme embodiment of the idea of the dignity of difference.

There is a Jewish prayer that contains the words *bore nefashot rabbot vechesronam*, 'who creates many kinds of soul and their deficiencies'. This is a strange phrase. Normally we thank God for what we have, not for what we lack: for our gifts, not our deficiencies. The explanation is that if each of us lacked nothing, we would never need anyone else. We would be solitaries, complete in ourselves. The very fact that we are different means that what I lack, someone else has, and what someone else lacks, I have.[42]

It was this that led, at the dawn of history, to the division of labour and the birth of trade. It brought people together in mutually beneficial exchange. If I am good at making axe-heads and you at catching fish, we both gain if I trade some of my axe-heads for some of your fish. David Ricardo's Law of Comparative Advantage showed that this remained true even if you are better at making axe-heads than I am – so long as you are better at fishing than axe-making, and I am better at axe-making than fishing. As long as we are each better at some things than others, we both gain by exchange, even if whatever you do, you do better than me.[43] Everyone has something to contribute, and everyone gains through the contribution of others.

Market exchange is the paradigm of the win-win scenario and the non-zero-sumness of human relationship. This has not merely economic but moral and spiritual consequence. Diversity, as Johannes Althusius explained in his *Politica* (1603), is the divine blessing at the core of our sociality:

> Clearly, man by nature is a gregarious animal born for cultivating society with other men ... [For this reason] God distributed his gifts unevenly among men. He did not give all things to one person, but some to one and some to others, so that you have need for my gifts, and I for yours. And so was born, as it were, the need for communicating necessary and useful things, which communication was not possible except in social and political life. God therefore willed that each need the service and aid of others in order that friendship would bind all together, and no one would consider another to be valueless. For if each did not need the aid of others, what would society be? What would reverence and order be? What would reason and humanity be? Everyone therefore needs the experience and contributions of others, and no one lives to himself alone.[44]

This means that human interaction is not inescapably tragic. It is not destined to be agonistic, conflictual, a matter of victory for some and defeat for others. I suspect that this is what differentiated biblical sensibility from that of ancient Greece. The Hellenistic world perfected the art of tragedy. By contrast, Judaism created a theology of hope. The fact that – individually, collectively, culturally – we are different can have two outcomes. It can lead to war, or it can lead to trade. Greece, with its military virtues, valued the manly arts of war. Jews, with their deep experience of suffering and exile, learned early to prefer peace.

Not the least contribution of market exchange to history is that it, more than any other institution, has been counterforce to the primordial human instinct to fight. Already in the eighteenth century, Montesquieu foresaw this: 'The natural effect of commerce is to lead to peace. Two nations that trade together become mutually dependent: if one has an interest in buying, the other has one in selling; and all unions are based on mutual needs.'[45] It is no small achievement that monetary union has brought together European nations whose conflicts in the past led to two world wars. Thomas Friedman coined what he calls the 'global arches' theory, that no two countries who have a McDonald's have ever fought a war against one another.[46]

In an age of resurgent tribalism, the global market offers – as trade has always done – an alternative script to difference as a source of conflict, and therefore tragedy. It turns difference into a form of blessing from which not only I, but others also, benefit. Adam Smith was not wrong when he invested the market with a quasi-religious significance in speaking of the 'invisible hand' by which our individual contributions combine to enhance the general wealth of nations. Economic virtues – hard work, inventiveness, the profit motive – have always seemed tame when set against the heroic virtues of military societies. But military societies kill. Wars destroy. Valour, courage, dying in a noble cause, seem heroic from the point of view of victors, but not from that of their victims.

If the price of war has become too high, which it has, we will have to value the habits of trade – the only thing that, throughout history, has brought tribes and nations together, benefiting from one another and from their several and different skills. The interlinking of nations in a network of trade causes many problems, to which I now turn. But it is also our last best hope for peace. Unlike the battlefield, the market is an arena in which both sides can win.

NOTES

1. Friedman 2000, pp. 101–11.
2. Soros 1998.
3. Babylonian Talmud, *Shabbat,* p. 119b.
4. *Mekhilta* to Exodus 15: 26.
5. Babylonian Talmud, *Baba Kamma*, p. 30a.
6. Weber 1985.
7. Novak 1993.
8. Wright 2000, pp. 156–8, 376–7.
9. Sombart 1997, p. 21.
10. See Buber 1996.
11. See Dennis and Halsey 1988; Dale 2000.
12. Plato, *The Republic*, Book IV, Chapter 2; 1955, pp. 161–5.
13. Aristotle, *The Politics*, p. 1328b41; 1988, p. 168.
14. Quoted in Hirschman 1997, p. 106.
15. See Acton 1993, pp. 32–3.
16. Quoted in Acton 1993, p. 57.
17. Landes 1998.
18. Mishnah *Avot (Ethics of the Fathers)*, 2: 2.
19. *Avot de Rabbi Natan*, Chapter 11.
20. Babylonian Talmud, *Berakhot*, p. 8a
21. Babylonian Talmud, *Pesachim*, p. 118a.
22. Rabbenu Bachya, *Kad hakemach*. Quoted in Tamari 1987, p. 31.
23. Maimonides, *Mishneh Torah*, Laws of Theft, 6: 8–11.
24. See Meilaender 2000, p. 6.
25. Tosefta, *Kiddushin*, 1: 11.
26. Maimonides, *Mishneh Torah*, Laws of Torah Study, 3: 10.1
27. See Stitskin 1982, p. 83.
28. Jerusalem Talmud, *Berakhot*, 9: 2.
29. *Mekhilta de-Rabbi Shimon bar Yochai*, 18: 13.

30. Midrash Tanchuma, *Tazria* to Leviticus 12: 3.
31. Quoted in Acton 1993, p. 45.
32. Weber 1952. See also Berger 1967.
33. Jerusalem Talmud, *Kiddushin*, 4: 12.
34. Deuteronomy 26: 11.
35. Babylonian Talmud *Nedarim*, 7b; *Baba Batra*, p. 116a; Exodus Rabbah 31: 14.
36. Smith 1986, Book 1, Chapter II, p. 119.
37. Smith 1937, p. 423.
38. Genesis Rabbah 9: 7.
39. Galbraith 1992.
40. Babylonian Talmud, *Baba Batra*, pp. 21a, 22a.
41. Novak 1992, p. 64.
42. I am indebted to Joshua Rowe of Manchester for this insight.
43. See Ridley 1996, pp. 207–9.
44. Althusius 1995, p. 23. A similar sentiment can be found in Jacques Savary's seventeenth-century business text, *Le Parfait négociant*: '[Divine providence] has not willed for everything that is needed for life to be found in the same spot. It has dispersed its gifts so that men would trade together and so that the mutual need which they have to help one another would establish ties of friendship between them' (quoted in Hirschman, 1997, pp. 59–60). Also see Adam Smith 1986, p. 121.
45. Quoted in Hirschman 1997, p. 80.
46. Friedman 2000, pp. 248–75. Friedman notes that since he first advanced this theory, there has been an exception: the 1999 NATO campaign in Kosovo.

Chapter 6

Compassion: The Idea of *Tzedakah*

> The great concern of Moses was ... to lay the foundation of
> a social state in which deep poverty and degrading want
> should be unknown.
>
> (Henry George, *Moses*)

'Think of a stretch limousine driving through an urban ghetto',
writes Martin Wolf of the *Financial Times*.[1] 'Inside is the postindustrial world of western Europe, North America, Australasia,
Japan and the emerging Pacific Rim. Outside are all the rest.'
That is what a globalized planet is rapidly becoming: one in
which wealth is ever more unevenly distributed, in which the rich
get richer and the poor get poorer. Each year there are more
billionaires. Each year millions die of starvation, poverty and
preventable disease. That is the difference between micro- and
macro-economics. In each individual transaction, both sides gain.
But when the results of billions of transactions are aggregated,
their effects can be, and often are, massively inequitable. That is
something globalization has magnified, not diminished. It turns
the planet into a single market with highly mobile funds and near-
perfect information and competition. Investment moves from
country to country, seeking maximal returns without regard to
human consequences. Our world is getting less equal by the year.

That inequality exists both within and between countries. In the second half of the twentieth century, worldwide consumption of goods and services grew six-fold. But according to a United Nations survey, one-sixth of the world's population – a billion people – live on less than a dollar a day and cannot satisfy the most basic human needs. More than eight million die each year because of polluted water or contaminated air. Six million die from malnutrition or starvation. Two million die from diarrhoea or related diseases.[2] AIDS has already claimed the lives of ten million Africans and is projected to kill 25 million more in the next decade. Among the 4.5 billion inhabitants of developing countries, three in five lack access to basic infrastructure. A third have no drinkable water. A quarter live in substandard accommodation. A fifth have no sanitary or medical services. In Africa, the poorest region of the world, 174 of every thousand children fail to reach the age of five. A fifth of the world's children spend less than five years in school. The same percentage are permanently undernourished.[3]

And the gap grows. Between 1965 and 1999, real incomes per head in the developed countries rose by 2.4 per cent. Those in the Middle East and North Africa stayed roughly the same. In sub-Saharan Africa they fell. Eighty-nine countries are worse off now than they were ten years ago. Thirty-five have experienced a greater fall than during the Great Depression of the 1930s. Worldwide, the top 20 per cent of high-income earners account for 86 per cent of all private consumption, while the poorest 20 per cent account for only 1.3 per cent. The richest fifth consume sixteen times more meat, seventeen times more energy and 145 times more cars than the poorest fifth. Of the world's total population, 65 per cent have never made a telephone call; 40 per cent have no access to electricity. Americans spend more on cosmetics, and Europeans on ice cream, than it would cost to provide schooling and sanitation for the two billion people who currently go without both.

In 1999 the United Nations Development Programme estimated that the world's three richest individuals had more assets than the 600 million who make up the world's poorest nations. The top 358 billionaires are collectively richer than almost a half of the earth's inhabitants combined. Meanwhile, aid from the developed countries remains exceptionally low. Only four Western countries – Denmark, Norway, Sweden and the Netherlands – reach the UN target of 0.7 per cent of national income. America, the world's richest nation, is at the bottom of the table, with 0.1 per cent. Yet, according to one calculation by the UN Development Programme, a mere 4 per cent of the wealth of the 225 richest individuals would be sufficient to provide elementary educational and medical facilities and adequate nutrition for all the world's poor.[4]

Within the developed countries themselves, disparities have grown to the point where income distribution is less equal than at any time since the early twentieth century. In the United States at the start of the 1990s, incomes of company directors were on average 42 times higher than those of blue-collar workers. Ten years later they were 419 times higher. Of the surplus of over a thousand billion dollars generated between 1979 and 1999, 95 per cent went to a mere 5 per cent of Americans. Between 1968 and 1998 the gap in earnings between the top 1 per cent and the middle increased five-fold. The new economy tends to reward the few while leaving those at the bottom with fewer chances of reasonably paid employment. As manufacturing is moved to low-income countries and agriculture no longer employs more than 2 per cent of the population, significant numbers of young people are left without the prospects they might have had a generation ago. The new meritocracy is ruthless in separating the winners from the losers.

In the most advanced economies, people are working harder with less security and a weaker safety-net than at any time in the recent past. The average American at the turn of the century worked the equivalent of two weeks a year more than he or she did ten years earlier. In the case of an average married couple with children, the figure is seven weeks. In 1969, 38 per cent of married mothers worked for pay. Thirty years later this figure had risen to 70 per cent. Making a living is at the top of young people's concerns. In 1968, 75 per cent of college freshmen listed 'developing a meaningful philosophy of life' as very important, while only 41 per cent said the same for 'being well-off financially'. Three decades later, the percentages had been reversed.[5] Meanwhile, new centres of poverty have emerged, particularly among single mothers and their children. Between the beginning of the 1980s and the end of the 1990s, child poverty in Britain doubled. A similar pattern has emerged in the United States. Typically, financial deprivation goes hand in hand with social poverty: depressed neighbourhoods, atrophying communities, high crime, drug-dealing, failing schools and overextended social services. Too many children in today's world, not only in the developing countries but also in run-down urban neighbourhoods in some of the richest nations on earth, are growing up without hope.

* * *

It is morally impossible not to be troubled by the ever-growing gap between the few at the top and the many at the bottom of the economic ladder. What makes the present situation worse than in the past is that these inequalities are visible. When the horizons of the majority of mankind were limited to the next village or town, inequalities might exist throughout the world, but few were aware of them on a daily basis. There were fabled lands where gold ran free, but that was somewhere else in the realm of legends and dreams. The global media have transformed all this. Television has brought the world of the rich and famous to the most remote villages, while bringing images of hunger, famine, war and disease into our living rooms. We can no longer claim that we did not know.

Nor are traditional defences of inequality sustainable today. The worldview of antiquity and the Middle Ages was built on the belief that differences in power, wealth and status were part of the ordained order. Status was a given of birth. Hierarchy was written into the fabric of the universe. Some, said Aristotle, are born to be free, while others are born to be slaves. True or not, said Plato, people must be trained to believe that differences in fate are preordained, if societies are to defend themselves against unrest: inequalities can be lamented but they cannot be changed. That canonization of the *status quo* has no place in the contemporary world. Modernity is the move from fate to choice, and we can no longer reasonably claim that the way things are is how they were destined to be.

Why then does it continue? Many defenders of the new economy argue – rightly, in my view – that it is the best chance nations have of defeating poverty. Countries that have embraced it, most notably in South East Asia, but also in South America, have prospered. So too has India, which has developed a highly effective information-technology base. The economic reforms introduced by Deng Xiaoping in China in 1978 helped 800 million peasants to double their incomes in a mere six years. Seventy-six million Chinese moved out of poverty in the past decade alone.[6]

But not every nation has access to the new technologies. They are on the other side of the so-called digital divide. Nor have world economic policies always been to the benefit of the poorest. Nobel prize-winning economist Joseph Stiglitz, former chief economist of the World Bank, has been highly critical of international financial institutions for the way they have imposed inappropriate strategies on failing economies. Economic liberalization can make the strong stronger but the weak weaker. Money is more mobile than people. Funds that flowed into a developing economy can equally rapidly flow out, leaving industries devastated and huge numbers of people unemployed. Speculative capital is not always invested in education and infrastructure. Often it is invested in sectors with quick gains, fuelling property booms while leaving long-term growth untouched. Stiglitz compares some of the economic policies imposed by the International Monetary Fund on poor countries to setting small boats loose on a rough sea. Even if the boats are sound and well-captained, they are likely to be hit broadside by a big wave and capsize.[7]

Nor has help always come from multinational corporations. They are not charged with the pursuit of justice. They exist to generate profits for shareholders, and that, by and large, is what they do. If currency movements or differential wage-rates mean that they can cut costs substantially by moving production from one country to another, they will do this. The costs in terms of local misery and disruption do not accrue to them. Even if they did, most multinationals have divested themselves of ownership of their manufacturing base, which is now contracted out. Corporate responsibility of first-world companies for third-world economies has become diffuse and easily evaded. Multinational firms have become the targets of a growing protest movement, documented in Naomi Klein's *No Logo*, by people rightly concerned at high-profit companies factoring out their production to countries where workers labour for long hours at low pay in insanitary conditions. There is a strong case for international regulation to improve wage-rates and work conditions. But there is also a convergence of interest between the corporations on the one hand, and governments seeking to attract investment on the other, leaving the workers themselves with little power to change their fate.

The other key players are nation-states themselves. But their commitment to international aid remains ambivalent, not least because often in the past it has failed to get through to people in need. It has been commandeered by governments, and sometimes used to prop up failing, oppressive and dictatorial regimes. In Africa, for example, 90 per cent of the hungry live in rural areas, but because the continent's political elite tend to live in port cities, the countryside suffers from neglect. As one aid worker put it during the 1984–85 famine, 'Starve the city people and they riot, starve the rural people and they die. If you were a political leader, which would you choose?'[8] During the 1990s there were seventeen major armed conflicts in Africa alone, as compared to ten elsewhere in the world, leaving 20 million people, mainly women and children, starving and in need of humanitarian assistance. Aid, to be effective, needs good government, but good government cannot be created by aid.

Inevitably, too, Western governments face a conflict of interests. Their first duty is to protect their own economies. There is a fear that assisting developing countries may damage domestic welfare. Under conditions of total mobility of production, work goes to countries with the lowest wage-rates. Employment is exported, which means, in the short term at least, that unemployment is imported. This may benefit some in the developed countries – the elites who run companies and design and market products. The losers are the traditional blue-collar workers, who have seen production shift from within to across national boundaries. Service industries in almost all the developed countries have expanded while numbers in manufacturing have fallen. Governments may think twice about creating a situation in which rising employment elsewhere leads to falling employment among their own constituents.

A world in which the few prosper and many starve, offends our deepest sense of fairness and human solidarity. You do not have to be a convinced egalitarian to know that disparities of this magnitude – vast, concentrated wealth alongside widespread suffering – is intolerable. The real problem, though, is one of responsibility. No one planned this outcome. It happened as a result of billions of transactions, investments and purchasing decisions. As Robert Reich reminds us:

> The emergence of the global, high-tech economy seems largely out of anyone's hands. One development seems to have sparked the next, without any clear decision having been made about consequences. No one explicitly decided that technologies of communication, transportation, and information would advance as quickly as they have. Or that these technologies would push the economy from large-scale production toward a wide array of innovative products and services, with easy switching to better ones ... Nor, especially, did anyone decide to accept the downsides of all this progress.[9]

The invisible hand – the unanticipated outcome of a myriad actions and reactions – is not always benign.

There are no easy solutions, but there are hard questions. What is our responsibility to humanity as a whole? What bonds of obligation link us to those with whom we do not share a country, a political structure, a language or culture? What proportion of our wealth, if any, are we duty-bound to share? The language of rights is not always helpful here, because rights presuppose a network of law and obligation that can implement them. A right is like a cheque: it has value only if there is bank and an account against which it can be drawn. Without that it is mere expectation without delivery. What then is the moral basis of global economic responsibility?

At this level, religious concepts are more helpful than narrowly political or economic ones. The central insight of monotheism – that if God is the parent of humanity, then we are all members of a single extended family – has become more real in its implications than ever before. The Enlightenment gave us the concept of universal rights, but this remains a 'thin' morality, stronger in abstract ideas than in its grip on the moral imagination. Far more powerful is the biblical idea that those in need are our brothers and sisters and that poverty is something we feel in our bones. Every year on Passover Jews eat the bread of affliction and the bitter herbs of slavery. On the festival of Sukkot, they leave the comfort of their homes to live in shacks – 'tabernacles' – as a reminder of what it feels like to be without a solid roof, exposed to the elements, living as millions do today in Calcutta or Caracas. The great faiths do more than give abstract expression to our shared humanity; they move us to action and give compelling shape to the claims of others upon us.

I want to examine the Jewish experience because it combines two elements that are particularly relevant to our present situation. On the one hand, as I showed in the previous chapter, Judaism is sympathetic to the free market and limited government as the best defences of individual liberty and creativity. On the other, it was aware from the days of Moses that an open economy does not guarantee just outcomes in the larger sense of a society in which everyone has the means of a dignified existence. This, to Moses and the prophets, was a matter of deep concern. In the words of one contemporary biblical scholar: 'From the start, Israel lived with a covenant charter which put optimum value on a people in egalitarian relations under one sovereign divine power.'[10] Early Israelite religion was the attempt to create a 'heterogeneous, classless, decentralized association of tribes conceived as a brotherhood – and at least in larger measure than in Canaanite society, as a sisterhood – of social, economic and political equals.'[11] That involved a commitment, one we can trace through biblical legislation and prophetic utterance, to an economic order that balanced freedom with equity. To understand it, we must first understand the idea contained in one of Judaism's key words.

* * *

In two verses in the Book of Genesis, God specifies the mission with which Abraham and his descendants are to be charged:

> Shall I hide from Abraham what I am about to do? Abraham will surely become a great and powerful nation, and all nations of the earth will be blessed through him. For I have chosen him so that he will direct his children and his household after him to keep the way of the Lord by doing what is right [*tzedakah*] and just [*mishpat*], so that the Lord will bring about for Abraham what He has promised him. (Genesis 18: 17–19)

The two words, *tzedakah* and *mishpat*, signify different forms of justice. *Mishpat* means retributive justice or the rule of law. A free society must be governed by law, impartially administered, through which the guilty are punished, the innocent acquitted and human rights secured. *Tzedakah*, by contrast, refers to distributive justice, a less procedural and more substantive idea.

It is difficult to translate *tzedakah* because it combines in a single word two notions normally opposed to one another, namely *charity* and *justice*. Suppose, for example, that I give someone £100. Either he is entitled to it, or he is not. If he is, then my act is a form of justice. If he is not, it is an act of charity. In English (as with the Latin terms *caritas* and *iustitia*) a gesture of charity cannot be an act of justice, nor can an act of justice be described as charity. *Tzedakah* is therefore an unusual term, because it means both.

113

It arises from the theology of Judaism, which insists on the difference between possession and ownership. Ultimately, all things are owned by God, creator of the world. What we possess, we do not own – we merely hold it in trust for God. The clearest example is the provision in Leviticus: 'The land must not be sold permanently because the land is Mine; you are merely strangers and temporary residents in relation to Me' (Leviticus 25: 23). If there were absolute ownership, there would be a difference between justice (what we are bound to give others) and charity (what we give others out of generosity). The former would be a legally enforceable duty, the latter, at most, a moral obligation, the prompting of benevolence or sympathy. In Judaism, however, because we are not owners of our property but merely guardians on God's behalf, we are bound by the conditions of trusteeship, one of which is that we share part of what we have with others in need. What would be regarded as charity in other legal systems is, in Judaism, a strict requirement of the law and can, if necessary, be enforced by the courts.

What *tzedakah* signifies, therefore, is what is often called 'social justice', meaning that no one should be without the basic requirements of existence, and that those who have more than they need must share some of that surplus with those who have less. This is absolutely fundamental to the kind of society the Israelites were charged with creating, namely one in which everyone has a basic right to a dignified life and to be equal citizens in the covenantal community under the sovereignty of God. So, for example, the covenant code specifies:

> Do not ill-treat a stranger [i.e. a non-Israelite] or oppress him, for you were strangers in the land of Egypt.
> Do not take advantage of a widow or orphan. If you do, and they cry out to Me, I will certainly hear their cry ...
> If you lend money to one of My people among you who is needy, do not be like a money-lender: charge him no interest.
> If you take your neighbour's cloak as a pledge, return it to him by sunset, because his cloak is the only covering he has

for his body. What else will he sleep in? When he cries out to
Me, I will hear, for I am compassionate. (Exodus 22: 21–7)

God, for the Israelites, was actively concerned in the economic
and political order, especially with those who, because they lacked
power, or even a 'voice', became the victims of injustice and
inequity:

> He upholds the cause of the oppressed,
> And gives food to the hungry.
> The Lord sets prisoners free.
> The Lord gives sight to the blind,
> The Lord lifts up those who are bowed down,
> The Lord loves the righteous.
> The Lord watches over the stranger,
> And sustains the fatherless and the widow,
> But He frustrates the way of the wicked. (Psalm 146: 7–9)

The society the Israelites were to construct would stand as a
living contrast to what they experienced in Egypt: poverty,
persecution and enslavement. Their release from bondage was
only the first stage on their journey to freedom. The second – their
covenant with God – involved collective responsibility to ensure
that no one would be excluded from the shared graciousness of the
community and its life. Hence the Bible's insistence that a free
society cannot be built on *mishpat*, the rule of law, alone. It
requires also *tzedakah*, a just distribution of resources. This view
has close affinities with Nobel Prize-winning economist Amartya
Sen's concept of 'development as freedom':

> The adult who lacks the means of having medical treatment
> for an ailment from which she suffers is not only prey to
> preventable morbidity and possibly escapable mortality, but
> may also be denied the freedom to do various things – for
> herself and for others – that she may wish to do as a
> responsible human being. The bonded labourer born into
> semi-slavery, the subjugated girl child stifled by a repressive

society, the helpless landless labourer without substantial means of earning an income are all deprived not only in terms of well-being, but also in terms of the ability to lead responsible lives, which are contingent on having certain basic freedoms. Responsibility *requires* freedom.[12]

Sen has, I believe, put it absolutely correctly. *Individual* freedom may be best described, as Isaiah Berlin argued, in terms of 'negative liberty', namely the absence of constraints (*chofesh* in biblical Hebrew). But *collective* freedom (*cherut* in Hebrew) is something else. It means, among other things, that my freedom is not bought at the price of yours. A society in which the few prosper but the many starve, in which some but not all have access to good education, health care, and other essential amenities, is not a place of liberty. That requires more than an absence of coercion. It involves the removal of barriers to the exercise of responsible citizenship: 'poverty as well as tyranny, poor economic opportunities as well as systematic social deprivation, neglect of public facilities as well as intolerance or overactivity of repressive states'.[13]

* * *

How was this achieved? The Bible is set in the context of a predominantly agrarian society, and its provisions are designed to address the kinds of poverty that arise in that environment. No one could be made to work on the seventh day, so that for one day each week all economic and political hierarchies were suspended. Various portions of the harvest were set aside for the poor – the corner of the field, the forgotten sheaf, and similar measures for other crops (Leviticus 19: 9–10; Deuteronomy 15: 1–2). On the third and sixth year of the seven-year agricultural cycle, the hungry were given a tenth of all produce (Deuteronomy 26: 12). On the seventh year, when no labour was permitted on the soil, produce belonged to everyone, 'so that the poor of your people may eat' (Exodus 23: 10). All outstanding debts were cancelled (Deuteronomy 15: 1–2). This last provision was open to circumvention, so the Bible warns explicitly against it:

Be careful not to harbour this wicked thought: 'The seventh year, the year for cancelling debts, is near', so that you do not show ill will towards your needy brother and give him nothing. He may then appeal to the Lord against you, and you will be found guilty of sin. Give generously to him and do so without a grudging heart; then because of this the Lord your God will bless you in all your work and in everything you put your hand to. There will always be poor people in the land. Therefore I command you to be open-hearted towards your brothers and towards the poor and needy in your land. (Deuteronomy 15: 9–11)

Indebtedness is a form of servitude. To ban loans altogether would condemn people to poverty and deprive them of the chance to start or sustain their own enterprise. That is why, from a biblical perspective, micro-lending of the kind currently under-taken by the World Bank, is essential. Nothing is more effective in alleviating poverty than giving individuals the chance to create small businesses. But to allow debts to accumulate is also wrong: the economic system must encourage freedom, not financial slavery. That is why periodic debt release is necessary. It enables people to begin again, freed of the burdens of the past. The Bible is candid in its appeal to the lenders. Not only is debt relief a moral duty. It is, in the long run, the key to collective prosperity ('the Lord your God will bless you in all your work').

A similar idea lies behind the institution of the Jubilee year. Everyone must have a share in the land. In the course of time, some – through poverty, bad harvests or other misfortunes – will be forced to sell. One year in 50, therefore, all land is to be returned to its original owners so that no one is denied his or her ancestral inheritance. The connection between economic equity and political freedom is explicit: 'Consecrate the fiftieth year and proclaim liberty throughout the land to all its inhabitants. It shall be a jubilee for you; then shall each of you return to his inheritance; then shall you return, each of you, to his family'. (Leviticus 25: 10).

What these periodic redistributions testify to is the biblical awareness that *an equitable distribution will not emerge naturally from the free working of the market alone.* It is no coincidence that the single most effective recent campaign for international debt relief – Jubilee 2000 – was drawn directly from the biblical idea of the Jubilee year. It also underlies Chancellor of the Exchequer Gordon Brown's proposal for a 'modern Marshall Plan' for the developing world.[14] The sabbatical and Jubilee years act as a corrective to the market by restoring a level playing field to those who have been forced to sell either their labour or their land. They break the cycle of poverty and dependence.

* * *

With the transition, some 2,000 years ago, from biblical to post-biblical Judaism, we find a greater emphasis on *tzedakah*, the direct provision of financial aid, as opposed to agricultural produce. Israel had become less of an agrarian economy, more a society of small businesses and trade, and rabbinic law is a systematic attempt to apply the principles of the Bible to new economic circumstances. Communal taxes were instituted. New forms of distribution were set up, among them the *tamchui* which distributed food daily, and the *kuppah* which weekly provided funds for those in need. The disbursement of *tzedakah* funds called for high standards of probity, so to be appointed as a distributor of communal funds became one of the highest accolades the community could give.

The key text here was Deuteronomy 15: 8, 'You shall open your hand wide to him [the poor person] and shall surely lend him sufficient for his need in that which he lacks.' The rabbis took this to include gifts as well as loans. More importantly they read it as offering a definition of the kinds of poverty they were called on to address:

> *Sufficient for his need* – means that you are commanded to maintain him, but you are not commanded to make him rich. *That which he lacks* – means even a horse to ride on and a slave to run before him. It is told of Hillel the elder [head of the Jewish community in the first century BCE] that he

118

bought for a certain poor man of good family a horse to ride on and a slave to run before him. On one occasion he could not find a slave to run before him, so he himself ran before him for three miles.[15]

There are two kinds of poverty according to this interpretation. The first ('sufficient for his need') refers to an absolute subsistence level. In Jewish law this was taken to include food, housing, basic furniture and if necessary, funds to pay for a wedding. The second ('that which he lacks') means relative poverty – relative, however, not to others but to the individual's own previous standard of living. This is the first indication of something which plays an important role in the rabbinic understanding of poverty. Over and above sheer physical needs is a psychological dimension. Poverty *humiliates*, and a good society will not allow humiliation.

Protecting dignity and avoiding humiliation was a systematic element of rabbinical law. So, for example, the rabbis ruled that even the richest should be buried plainly so as not to shame the poor. On certain festive days girls, especially those from wealthy families, had to wear borrowed clothes, 'so as not to shame those who do not have'. The rabbis intervened to lower the prices of religious necessities so that no one would be excluded from communal celebrations. Work conditions had to be such that employees were treated with basic respect. Here, the proof text was God's declaration, 'For to Me the children of Israel are servants' – meaning that they were not to be treated as servants of any human being. Freedom presupposes self-respect, and a free society will therefore be one that robs no one of that basic human entitlement.

One element of self-respect is independence. This explains a remarkable feature of *tzedakah* legislation. Maimonides lists the various levels of giving-to-others, all except one of which involve philanthropy. The supreme act, however, does not:

The highest degree, exceeded by none, is that of one who assists a poor person by providing him with a gift or a loan or by accepting him into a business partnership or by helping him find employment – in a word by putting him in a situation where he can dispense with other people's aid. With reference to such aid it is said, 'You shall strengthen him, be he a stranger or a settler, he shall live with you' (Leviticus 25: 35), which means strengthen him in such a manner that his falling into want is prevented.[16]

This ruling is the result of a profound wrestling, within Judaism, with the fact that aid in the form of charity can itself be humiliating for the recipient. It can also create welfare dependency, reinforcing, not breaking the cycle of deprivation. The greatest act of *tzedakah* is therefore one that allows the individual to become self-sufficient. The highest form of aid is one that enables the individual to dispense with aid. Humanitarian relief is essential in the short term, but in the long run, job creation and the promotion of employment are more important.

There is one other detail of Jewish law which is particularly fascinating. It specifies that even a person dependent on *tzedakah* must himself or herself give *tzedakah*. On the face of it, the rule is absurd. Why give X enough money so that he can give to Y? Giving to Y directly is more logical and efficient. What the rabbis understood, however, is that *giving is an essential part of human dignity*. As an African proverb puts it: the hand that gives is always uppermost; the hand that receives is always lower. The rabbinic insistence that the community provide the poor with enough money so that they themselves can give is a profound insight into the human condition.

*   *   *

Judaism represents a highly distinctive approach to the idea of equality, namely that it is best served not by equality of income or wealth, nor even of opportunity. Nor is it sufficient that we each have equal standing before God at times of prayer, and before the law in cases of dispute. A society must ensure equal dignity – the Hebrew phrase is *kavod habriyot*, 'human honour' – to each of its members.

This is a constant theme of the prophets. Amos, one of the first literary prophets, says in his most famous oracle, 'They sell the righteous for silver, and the needy for a pair of shoes. They trample on the heads of the poor as upon the dust of the ground, and deny justice to the oppressed.' Isaiah says:

> The Lord enters into judgement with the elders and princes of His people: 'It is you who have devoured the vineyard, the spoil of the poor is in your houses. What do you mean by crushing My people, by grinding the face of the poor?' says the Lord God of hosts.

Jeremiah says simply of the reforming king Josiah, 'He judged the cause of the poor and needy; then it was well. Is this not to know Me? says the Lord.'

The prophets, who lived and worked more than 2,500 years ago, were the world's first social critics, unashamed to deliver their message to kings and speak truth to power. Religion has, they argued, a moral, social and economic dimension. It involves justice, not merely in the narrow sense of the rule of law and the transparency of procedures, but also in the substantive sense of conferring on all members of society an honoured place. Prophetic teaching, writes Johannes Lindblom, 'is characterized by the principle of solidarity. Behind the demand for charity and justice ... lies the idea of the *people*, the people as an organic whole, united by election and covenant.'[17] Huge disparities of wealth, exploitative practices, harsh conditions of employment, the existence of what some today call an 'underclass' – these are fractures in human solidarity. They create a divided society. They destroy the notion of the common good as something we share and in which we all participate. That is not something from which we can hide on the grounds that it is not our responsibility. As A. J. Heschel notes: '[T]he prophets remind us of the moral state of a people: Few are guilty but all are responsible. If we admit that the individual is in some measure conditioned or affected by the spirit of society, an individual's crime discloses society's corruption.'[18] And what in the days of the prophets applied socially, today applies globally. The scope of our interconnectedness defines the radius of responsibility and concern.

* * *

Tzedakah is a concept for our time. The retreat, set in motion by Reagonomics and Thatcherism, from a welfare state, together with the deregulation of financial markets throughout the world, has led to increased and increasing inequalities both in developed countries and the developing world. The importance of *tzedakah* is that it does not mean 'charity'. It is not optional, nor does it depend on the goodwill of those who give to others. It is a legally enforceable obligation. Nor does it depend on any specific economic doctrine. It goes hand in hand with a free market, while recognizing that the market has inherent limits. George Soros is right when he admits that

> International trade and global financial markets are very good at generating wealth, but they cannot take care of other social needs, such as the preservation of peace, alleviation of poverty, protection of the environment, labor conditions, or human rights – what are generally called 'public goods'.[19]

The inequities of markets are no reason to abandon the market. Globalization has led to increased prosperity for those countries which have participated in it. We will not cure poverty by destroying a system of wealth-creation, any more than we will cure illness by abolishing doctors or end crime by annulling law. New technologies and the growth of trade are our best – our only – hope for ending hunger, curing disease, and raising living standards throughout the world. This, the rabbis recognized. The Talmud imagines the following dialogue between King David and his advisers:

> At dawn, the wise men of Israel came to David and said, 'O Lord, the king, your people Israel need sustenance.' He said, 'Let them support one another.' They replied, 'A handful cannot satisfy a lion, and you cannot fill a pit by the earth which you dig from it.'[20]

David proposed redistribution. His sages told him that the cake was not big enough, however it was sliced. Economic growth is more powerful than simple redistribution. But that is true only if there is a genuine willingness on the part of those who gain to ensure that the losers also benefit; and that does not happen through the market mechanism on its own.

No religion can propose precise policies for the alleviation of hunger and disease. What it can do, and must, is to inspire us collectively with a vision of human solidarity and with concepts, such as *tzedakah* within the Jewish tradition and its counterparts in other faiths, that serve as a broad moral template for what constitutes a fair and decent world. Globalization, writes Zygmunt Bauman, 'divides as much as it unites ... signalling a new freedom for some, upon many others it descends as an uninvited and cruel fate'.[21] There can be no doubt that more – much more – of the economic surplus of advanced economies should be invested in developing countries to help eradicate extremes of poverty and hunger, ensure universal education, combat treatable disease, reduce infant mortality, improve work conditions and reconstruct failing economies. As with *tzedakah*, the aim should be to restore dignity and independence to nations as well as individuals. This has now become an urgent imperative. The globalization of communications, trade and culture, globalizes human responsibility likewise. The freedom of the few may not be purchased at the price of the enslavement of the many to poverty, ignorance and disease.

NOTES

1. *Financial Times*, 6 November 2001.
2. Micklethwait and Woolridge 2001, p. 256.
3. Zygmunt Bauman, 'Whatever Happened to Compassion', in Bentley and Stedman-Jones 2001, pp. 51–6.
4. Held and McGrew 2000, pp. 341–47.
5. Reich 2001, p. 124.
6. Micklethwait and Woolridge 2001, p. 259.
7. Joseph Stiglitz, 'Globalism's Discontents', *The American Prospect*, 13.1. (1 January 2002–14 January 2002).

8. Susan Sechler, 'Starved for Attention,' *The American Prospect*, 13.1 (1 January 2002–14 January 2002).
9. Reich 2001, p. 230.
10. Gottwald 1980, p. 699.
11. Ibid., p. 700.
12. Sen 1999, p. 284.
13. Ibid., p. 3.
14. Brown 2002.
15. Babylonian Talmud, *Ketubot*, p. 67b.
16. Maimonides, *Mishneh Torah*, Gifts to the Poor, 10: 7.
17. Lindblom 1962, p. 344.
18. Heschel 1962, p. 16.
19. Soros 2002, p. 14.
20. Babylonian Talmud, *Berakhoto* 3b.
21. Bauman 1998, p. 2.

Chapter 7

Creativity: The Imperative of Education

> Technologies are not mere exterior aids but also interior transformations of consciousness, and never more so than when they affect the word.
>
> (Walter J. Ong, *Orality and Literacy*)

Every invention changes the human environment, but none so fundamentally as those that change the way we record and transmit information. Other technologies have localized impacts; the effects of revolutions in information technology are systemic. They alter the most fundamental structures of society. They even change the way we speak and think, how we structure experience and make sense of it. Having argued, in the previous chapter, that *tzedakah* – the Jewish understanding of social justice – is about alleviating poverty in a way that makes for self-respect and independence, I want in this chapter to identify the single most effective way of doing so. Information technology, I will argue, is more than a technology: it has a profound impact on the democratization of human dignity. There is a story to be told about personal computers, modems, e-mail and the Internet that is, in its way, both spiritual and political and a source of genuine hope.

There have been three great information revolutions in the

125

past, and we are living through the fourth. Because the impact of the present transformation will not be known for decades, even centuries, to come, the best way of signalling the possibilities it may open up is to chart the history of the previous three. The best starting point is 31 October 1517, when the young Martin Luther nailed his 95 theses to the door of All Saints Church in Wittenberg, setting in motion the Reformation and a whole series of interconnected developments that led not only to religious reform but to a redrawing of the political map of Europe, the growth of science, the development of the nation-state and, in the broadest sense, the 'birth of the modern'. One of the stranger facts about that history is that some of the main features of the Reformation had already been set out by John Wycliffe in Oxford in the fourteenth century. Why was it that when he advocated change, little happened, but when Luther did likewise two centuries later, the tremors spread to virtually every country in the West?

The answer, of course, is that between them lay the invention of printing, by Johannes Gutenberg in Germany in the 1450s (printing had been invented in China several centuries earlier, but had not spread). It was one thing to urge Christians to go back to the Bible – *sola scriptura* – quite another for that to be practically possible in an age when books were handwritten and beyond the reach of most people. No sooner had printing been developed, than Bibles started flying from the presses in their hundreds of thousands. In England alone, it has been estimated that more than a million Bibles and New Testaments were published between the Reformation and 1640. Initially, Tyndale's New Testament cost three shillings, a significant sum, but the manuscripts it replaced cost between seven and eighteen times as much, and as time proceeded and competition increased, prices fell steadily. Luther's own declaration was transmitted by the press. Within fifteen days it had appeared throughout the country, and within three weeks, printing presses in three different towns were turning out copies. One sixteenth-century writer said that 'It almost appeared as if the angels themselves had been their messengers and brought them before the eyes of all the people.'

Between 1518 and 1525 Luther's writings accounted for no less than a third of all German-language books, and by 1546 a total of 430 separate editions of his biblical translations had appeared in print.[1]

Nothing did more to challenge ecclesiastical authority than the fact that the Bible in vernacular translation was now readily available to large masses of people, who could read and debate its words in the privacy of their homes. Many of the early Protestants attributed 'this gift of printing' to divine providence, and certainly its timing was providential and its effects tumultuous. Soon, though, even they began to realize that it was capable of undermining not one authority but all. Printing became, in the words of one commentator, 'the principal natural ally of libertine, heterodox and ecumenical philosophers'. One utopian pamphlet, *Macaria*, published in 1641, predicted that 'The art of printing will so spread knowledge that the common people, knowing their own rights and liberties, will not be governed by way of oppression.' Writing after the English Revolution, the poet Andrew Marvell imagined a future bishop saying to himself that

> the press ... hath done much more mischief to the discipline of our church than all the doctrine can make amends for. 'Twas an happy time when all learning was in manuscript, and some little officer ... did keep the keys of the library ... But now a man cannot write a book, but presently he is answered ... There have been ways found out to banish ministers, but no art yet could prevent these seditious meetings of letters.[2]

Printing had almost incalculable consequences. No invention had spread so rapidly before. By 1500, less than half a century after its inception, there were 35,000 separate titles in print, and between fifteen and twenty million books in circulation. By the end of the next century, that number had multiplied tenfold. Print was a huge boost to literacy. The more books were available, the more people learned to read, and the more they read, the more books they bought. The press provided new

127

channels of communication for governments and new ways of spreading artistic and architectural ideas. It enhanced the growth of science and the spread of technology. By encouraging the use of the vernacular and displacing Latin as the language of scholars, by diminishing the effects of dialect and standardizing spelling, it played a critical role in the growth of European languages and thus, ultimately, of national consciousness.

Benedict Anderson goes further.[3] The invention of printing, he argues, led to three fundamental shifts in people's view of the world. Firstly, it broke the medieval idea of a sacred script – the idea that there is one language (Church Latin, Qur'anic Arabic or Examination Chinese) that uniquely describes the true nature of reality. The multiplicity of printed languages, and especially published accounts of the great maritime journeys of discovery in the fifteenth and sixteenth centuries, familiarized people with the sheer variety of cultures. Secondly, the diffusion of reading led to the collapse of strictly hierarchical societies in which only a few were literate and had access to texts. Thirdly, it led to a new awareness of time. In the religion-dominated Middle Ages, time was relatively foreclosed. Whatever happened had already been prefigured in sacred texts. With the appearance of the first news pamphlets in the early sixteenth century, time – signalled by the date at the top of the paper – became a kind of empty medium in which events unfolded, in which 'news' happens. Hegel wryly noted that newspapers had become, for modern man, the substitute for morning prayers. The printing press, in short, changed the human landscape not only externally but internally also. More than any other invention it paved the way for the transition from the medieval to the modern age.

* * *

No less dramatic was the first revolution: the invention of writing itself. Art – the pictorial representation of things seen – appeared relatively early in the cultural evolution of mankind. The earliest cave paintings, dating back some 20 to 30 thousand years, are still astonishing in their vitality. Over time, some of these representations became more schematic, a matter of a few strokes and geometrical patterns. Memory devices also appeared early – knots in cords, notches in sticks, marks on stones, tokens and other *aides-mémoire*. Writing as such, however, did not appear until the people known as the Sumerians entered southern Mesopotamia during the fourth millennium BCE.[4]

We do not know precisely how and when it emerged, but it was almost certainly a byproduct of new building materials, specifically the making of bricks from clay tablets dried in the sun. Marks made by a wedge-shaped stick while the clay was still wet would become indelible once the tablet had become hard and could thus serve as permanent records. The first signs to be inscribed were pictographic – no more than schematic representations of objects. But the technique developed rapidly into a system not of representation but communication. Symbols were strung together in linear sequences and became phonetic, standing not for objects but for sounds. The wedge-shaped sticks used to make impressions in the clay gave this first of written languages its name: cuneiform.

The settlement of populations, the development of agriculture and the birth of complex economies with their division of labour and growth of exchange, gave writing its earliest and most immediately practical use, namely to record transactions. But the power of the system was soon apparent. It could do more than keep a note of who owed what to whom. It could capture for posterity the great narratives – myths, cosmologies and epic histories – that explained the present in terms of the past, and whose telling in oral form had been a central feature of ancient religious rituals. While cuneiform was being developed, a parallel process was taking place in ancient Egypt, giving rise to the family of scripts known as hieroglyphics. In all, writing may have been invented independently as many as seven times – in India, China and Greece (Minoan or Mycenean 'Linear B') and later by the Mayans and Aztecs as well in the ancient Mesopotamian city-states and the Egypt of the Pharaohs.[5]

The birth of writing was the genesis of civilization. For the first time knowledge could be accumulated and handed on to future generations in a way that exceeded, in quantity and quality, the scope of unaided memory. Few things have been more significant for the development of *homo sapiens*, the being whose period of dependency is longer, and whose genetically encoded instincts are fewer, than any other. Humanity's great evolutionary advantage is that we are, *par excellence*, the learning animal. Writing was the breakthrough by which the present could hand on the lessons of the past to the generations of the future. It led to a quantum leap in the growth of knowledge and skills, and to a huge acceleration in the pace of change in human affairs.

As would happen later in the case of printing, writing had internal as well as external reverberations. In Walter J. Ong's phrase, 'writing restructures consciousness'.[6] An oral culture is one in which the communication of knowledge always has a human context. There is a speaker, an audience and an occasion. Writing, by contrast, is context-free. The writer does not necessarily know who will read what he has written, nor does the reader usually have the writer present in person to explain what he or she meant. Plato, in the *Phaedrus*, has Socrates object to the whole practice of writing. It will lead, he says, to a loss of memory, to a more passive form of learning, and to endless disputation, since what one writer has written, another can challenge, without either of them meeting and arguing the issue to a conclusion. Certainly writing was a huge move in the direction of abstraction. Speech is natural in the sense that every human group has it. Writing is artificial. It needs rules and conventions and these must be consciously learned. But it also facilitates abstract thought and it tends to fix the past in ways that oral cultures – who know their past through constant retelling – have no way of doing.

The early forms of writing, however, suffered from one significant disadvantage. Because each character represented a word or syllable, their symbol-sets were large. The time it took to master them – to learn to read and write – was such that literacy was bound to remain the preserve of a cognitive elite, a knowledge class. The extreme case is Chinese. The K'anghsi dictionary of 1716 lists 40,545 characters. To know them all is almost impossible. To become adept in the written language took on average twenty years. The first forms of writing therefore exemplify Bacon's famous observation that knowledge is power. With literacy available only to the few – an administrative class, usually the priesthood – the result was a series of stratified societies in which knowledge was not widely diffused and most people had no access to education and information.

That is what makes the second revolution in information technology – the invention of the alphabet – so significant. It was far more than a technical advance. It heralded far-reaching social and political possibilities. For the first time the entire universe of communicable knowledge was reduced to a symbol-set of between 20 and 30 letters, small enough to be mastered, at least in principle, by everyone. Again, origins are shrouded in mystery, but we know that the first alphabetical scripts were Semitic and that they emerged in the territory known today as Israel or to the south of it, in the Sinai Desert. The most likely hypothesis is that the alphabet evolved as a simplified form of the Egyptian hieroglyphic script or its abbreviated cursive form, known as hieratic. The inventors may have been Canaanites or Phoenicians or the wandering folk known as Apiru, from which the word 'Hebrew' may be derived.

The alphabet appeared early in the second pre-Christian millennium, in the age of the biblical patriarchs.[7] There is evidence from the turquoise mines of Serabit in the Sinai Desert that it was there, among the slave workers or their supervisors, that the breakthrough came. William Flinders Petrie, the British archaeologist of the early twentieth century, went so far as to speculate that the first alphabetical scripts were used by the Israelites while they were slaves in Egypt or later on their way to the promised land. Be that as it may, the alphabet was one of those rare inventions that happened only once in history. Unlike writing, which appeared independently in several civilizations, all alphabetical systems in use today derive directly or indirectly from the first 'proto-Sinaitic' scripts. To be sure, it was not until they were transferred, probably by trading Phoenicians, to Greece, that for the first time symbols were added to represent vowels (Hebrew to this day is a consonantal script). But the Semitic origin of the alphabet is still evident in the word itself: a combination of the first two Hebrew letters, *aleph* and *bet* (*alpha-beta* in Greek).

* * *

The alphabet created the possibility of profound social and political change. As already noted, the pre-alphabetical world was, and could not be other than, hierarchical. At the apex of Mesopotamian or Egyptian society was a ruler, king or pharaoh, seen as a god, or child of the gods, or the prime intermediary between the people and the gods. Below him and holding much of the day-to-day power was the cognitive elite, the administrative class. Below them was the mass of the people, conceived as a vast work- or military force. The cultures of the ancient world were mythological, or what Eric Voegelin called 'cosmological'.[8] What this meant was that the divisions in society were seen as mirroring the hierarchy of the gods or planets or elemental forces. They were written into the structure of the universe itself. Nor was this an abstract idea. It was made visible in the monumental architecture of the age – the ziggurats of Babylon and the pyramids and temples of pharaonic Egypt, each a statement in stone of the power structure of antiquity. William Shakespeare has left us a memorable statement of this kind of worldview:

> The heavens themselves, the planets, and this centre,
> Observe degree, priority, and place,
> Insisture, course, proportion, season, form,
> Office, and custom, in all line of order ...
> Take but degree away, untune that string,
> And, hark, what discord follows![9]

This is, needless to say, a deeply conservative vision, a view of society in which the individual's status is a given of birth and cannot be changed without disturbing the fundamental order on which the world depends.

By contrast, the invention of the alphabet heralded an entirely new possibility, namely of a society in which each individual has access to knowledge, and thus power, and hence ultimate dignity in the presence of God. A world of potential universal literacy is one in which everyone has claim to citizenship under the sovereignty of God. That is the significance of the most revolutionary of all religious utterances, the declaration in the first chapter of Genesis that not only kings and pharaohs but every human being is God's 'image and likeness'. Though it would take thousands of years for it to work its way into the culture of the West, it is here that the idea is first given expression that would become, in the American Declaration of Independence, the famous statement: 'We hold these truths to be self-evident, that all men are created equal, that they are endowed by their Creator with certain unalienable rights, that among these are Life, Liberty and the pursuit of Happiness . . .' The irony is that these truths are anything *but* self-evident. They are the negation of a view, held almost universally in the ancient world, given philosophical expression by Plato and Aristotle, and maintained throughout the Middle Ages, that people are *not* born equal. Some are born to be rulers, others to be ruled.

* * *

The politics of ancient Israel begins with an act inconceivable to the cosmological mind, namely that God, creator of the universe, intervenes in history to *liberate slaves*. It reaches a climax in the nineteenth chapter of the Book of Exodus with an event unique in religious history, in which God reveals Himself to an entire people at Mount Sinai and enters into a covenant with them. The passage is full of interest, but its significance has rarely been properly understood. We tend to think of revelatory moments as belonging to something narrowly defined as 'religion'. The Sinai covenant, however, rightly belongs to the political as much as the religious history of the West. These are the key verses:

> Then Moses went up to God, and the Lord called to him from the mountain and said, 'This is what you are to say to the house of Jacob and tell to the people of Israel: "You yourselves have seen what I did to Egypt, and how I carried

you on eagles' wings and brought you to myself. Now if you obey me fully and keep my covenant, then out of all nations you will be my treasured possession. Although the whole earth is mine, you will be for me a kingdom of priests and a holy nation." These are the words you are to speak to the Israelites.' ... The people all responded together, 'We will do everything the Lord has said.' (Exodus 19: 3–8)

Only then does God declare the Ten Commandments.

What is happening in this encounter? A covenant is being made which turns the Israelites from a people linked by history and biological descent into a body politic under the sovereignty of God. The idea of covenant did not originate with the Israelites.[10] It was a standard form of treaty between neighbouring powers in the ancient Near East. It was, however, taken over by the Hebrew Bible and given an entirely new and theological dimension. Three things about the Sinai covenant are revolutionary. The first is that one of the partners is God himself. The idea that God might bind himself to a formal agreement with a group of human beings was unprecedented. It was the theological precursor of constitutional monarchy. The second is that the other partner is not – as in all other ancient treaties – a leader or king, but the entire people, each one of whom, by being given the right of assent or refusal, is granted the dignity of citizenship. The third is that God, by inviting the people to signal their willingness to enter the covenant before communicating its terms, is in effect making it conditional on their agreement. To put it in the language of the American Declaration of Independence: there is no legitimate government without 'the consent of the governed', even when the governor is Creator of heaven and earth! Here, even more than in the city-states of ancient Greece, is born the idea of a free society.

Never before, and rarely since, has the dignity of the human person in the presence of God – the citizen of the nation of faith under Divine sovereignty – been so singularly elevated. My argument is that this remarkable phenomenon is intimately related to the invention of the alphabet. The idea that everyone might learn to read and write and thus have access to knowledge creates, for the first time in history, the possibility of universal citizenship. I would go further. There is, in the passage quoted above, a strange and not immediately intelligible phrase. Israel is called on to be 'a kingdom of priests'. In fact, in any literal sense, this never happened. The priesthood in ancient Israel was confined to Aaron and his sons. However in most premodern societies the priesthood had one notable characteristic. Priests could read and write. The word 'hieroglyphic' means 'priestly script'. To this day, the word 'clerical' in English has a double meaning, 'related to the clergy' and 'pertaining to a clerk or scribe' – a relic of the Middle Ages when ministers of religion held a near-monopoly of education. Understood functionally, therefore, the phrase 'a kingdom of priests' means *a society of universal literacy*. Ancient Israel may or may not have invented the alphabet, but more than any other people, they meditated deeply on the new social and political possibility it heralded, of a society predicated on education and universal access to knowledge.

The Israel of Moses and the prophets was the not always successful, but none the less historically unprecedented attempt to envisage and create a society as a covenant of equal citizens freely bound to one another and to God. As Norman Gottwald puts it, the God of Israel was:

> the historically concretized, primordial power to establish and sustain social equality in the face of counter-oppression from without and against provincial and nonegalitarian tendencies from within the society ... Israel thought it was different because it was different: it constituted an egalitarian social system in the midst of stratified societies.[11]

This, I have suggested, would have been impossible without the existence of the alphabet, which for the first time made universal literacy a conceivable idea. The alphabet gave rise to the book and thus to the people of the book.

* * *

I have told this story at length to convey something of the moral

135

and political drama that accompanies changes in information technology. We miss their significance when we think of them on an analogy with other technological transformations. Changes in the way we record and transmit information have deep effects, few of which are apparent at the time, but which are among the most potent in the history of civilization. They transform habits of the mind, structures of the imagination, and the way we order our common life. There have been three such revolutions in the past – writing, the alphabet and the invention of printing – and we are living through the fourth: instantaneous global communication. We do not yet know, and will not for centuries, what its cumulative consequences will be. Will it spell the end, or at least the decline, of the nation-state? Will it lead to new forms of community and collaborative action? Will it hasten the demise of local languages in favour of the dominant tongue of the Internet, American-English? Will it bring about a fundamental reorienta- tion of human consciousness, reducing the significance of space in favour of time? One thing is certain: the changes will go deep and they will be, among other things, 'spiritual'. Writing gave birth to civilization. The alphabet gave rise to monotheism. Printing made the Reformation possible. Precisely because religion tracks the deepest connections between self, the other and the universe, it is sensitive to transformations of this kind. New communication technologies make possible new modes of relationship, new social, economic and political structures, and thus new ways of under- standing the human situation under God.

This has an immediate implication for the ethics of globaliza- tion. The best investment developed nations can make in the developing world – and developing economies themselves – is to ensure that every child has maximal opportunity for learning. Education is still far too unevenly distributed. Of the world's children, 113 million do not go to school. On present projections, 88 countries will not achieve primary education for all by 2015. There are 23 countries – mostly in Africa, but they include Afghanistan, Bangladesh, Nepal, Pakistan and Haiti – in which half or more of the adult population are illiterate. In 35 countries – including Algeria, Egypt, Guatemala, India, Laos, Morocco,

Nigeria and Saudi Arabia – half or more women cannot read or write. Compared to North America, Latin America suffers a 50 per cent higher poverty rate and a 70 per cent greater high school drop-out rate. Within the United States itself, Hispanics are significantly poorer and less educated than other groups.[12] There is a high correlation between education and economic achievement: it has been estimated that every additional year of schooling in a poor country adds between 10 and 20 per cent to a child's eventual income.

Education – the ability not merely to read and write but to master and apply information and have open access to knowledge – is essential to human dignity. I have suggested that it is the basis of a free society. Because knowledge is power, equal access to knowledge is a precondition of equal access to power. It is also the key to *creativity*, and creativity is itself one of the most important gifts with which any socioeconomic group can be endowed. More than that, it has become the key to flourishing in the twenty-first century.

In ancient times, wealth and power lay in the ownership of persons, usually slaves. In the feudal era they took the form of ownership of land. In the industrial age they went with ownership of capital and the means of production. In the information age they lie in access to and deployment of intellectual capital, the ability to master information and turn it to innovative ends – what Joseph Nye calls 'soft' power.[13] The labour content of manufactured goods continues to fall. Huge profits go to those who have ideas. To an ever-increasing degree, multinational corporations are outsourcing production and peripheral services and becoming, instead, owners of concepts: brands, logos, images and designs.[14] In such an economy, immense advantages accrue to those with intellectual and creative skills. Education, not merely basic but extended, becomes a necessity, even a fundamental human right. Investment in education is the most important way in which a society offers its children a future.

So fundamental has this idea been to Judaism that it might in fairness be called a faith predicated on education. Moses instructs the Israelites, 'Teach these things diligently to your children,

137

speaking of them when you sit at home and when you walk on the road, when you lie down and when you rise up'(Deuteronomy 6: 7). Returning to Israel from Babylon in the fifth century BCE, Ezra assembles the people at one of the gates of Jerusalem and reinstates the teaching of the Law in a vast ceremony of adult education: 'They read from the Book of the Law of God, making it clear and giving the meaning so that the people could understand what was being read' (Nehemiah 8: 8).

Ezra became a new archetype: the teacher as hero. From then on, Judaism steadily evolved the institutions – schools, houses of study, and the synagogue as a house not only of prayer but also of public reading and explanation of the Torah – that were to sustain it after the fall of the Second Temple and the global dispersion of Jewry. By the first century CE, Josephus writes that 'should any one of our nation be asked about our laws, he will repeat them as readily as his own name. The result of our thorough education in our laws from the very dawn of intelligence is that they are, as it were, engraved on our souls.'[15] H. G. Wells observed that 'the Jewish religion, because it was a literature-sustained religion, led to the first efforts to provide elementary education for *all* the children in the community'.[16]

Universal literacy is a relatively recent idea in the West. Compulsory education was not instituted in Britain until 1870. Jewry seems to have been unique in instituting and sustaining it throughout most of its history. There is evidence from the Book of Judges that as early as 1000 BCE much, even most, of the population could read and write. A complete school system, primary and secondary, was in place by the first century. One provision from the Middle Ages gives a sense of the nature of communal provision.

The Jews of Spain in the fifteenth century were a community in distress. They had experienced their equivalent of Kristallnacht – burning and looting of synagogues, Jewish businesses and homes – in 1391, and were subjected to persecution for a century until their expulsion in 1492. In the midst of this experience they decided that whatever else might suffer, children should not be denied the best possible education. The Valladolid synod of 1432 imposed special taxes on meat and wine, together with levies on weddings, circumcisions and burials, all of which went to fund schooling. The assembly ordained

> that every community of fifteen householders [or more] shall be obliged to maintain a qualified elementary teacher to instruct their children in Scripture. They shall provide him with sufficient income for a living in accordance with the number of his dependants. The parents shall be obliged to send their children to that teacher, and each shall pay him in accordance with his means. If this revenue from the parents should prove inadequate, the community shall be obliged to supplement it with an amount necessary for his livelihood in accordance with the time and place.[17]

Already in the third century the rabbis had ruled that any Jewish community that failed to establish a school was to be excommunicated. Throughout the centuries, when the vast majority of Europe was illiterate, Jews maintained an educational infrastructure as their highest priority. It is no exaggeration to say that this lay at the heart of the Jewish ability to survive catastrophe, negotiate change and flourish in difficult circumstances.

* * *

Much of the debate about globalization focuses on political and economic issues: global governance and the impact of the new economy. A Jewish perspective would argue that, vital though these are, the provision of universal education is more important still. In the foreseeable future, much will depend on the degree to which people are positioned to take advantage of new opportunities, and this in turn will depend on the extent and depth of investment in education. In fact, so rapidly are technologies changing that the idea that education is confined to childhood will have to be revised in favour of lifelong learning, itself a classic value of the Judaic tradition. Jewry is one of the paradigm cases of a group that predicated the idea of a society of equal human dignity not on the distribution of wealth or power but on access to education; and it worked.

That, I have argued, was itself the result of a revolution in information technology almost four millennia ago: the invention of the alphabet. The revolution we are living through – of personal computers, modems, e-mails, interactive CD-ROMs and the Internet – should be understood in the same terms. Their ultimate significance is their contribution to the *democratization of knowledge*, and thus of dignity and creativity. The first imperative of the new information technology should be to make available to every child the universe of knowledge opened up by instantaneous global communication.

One model here is the Bôlsa-Escola scheme in Brazil that provides subsidies to poor families provided that their children attend school regularly. School participation in Brazil has risen, as a result, to 97 per cent of the child population.[18] Recently, at a special session of the United Nations General Assembly,[19] Britain backed a World Bank initiative to provide the funds to ensure universal primary education throughout the world by 2015. This is the correct prioritization. The more education children have, the wider their employment prospects, the more they are able to earn, and the more effectively they are able to cope with rapidly changing economic circumstances. The Internet has widened the availability and lowered the cost of tuition at all levels. Curricula can be designed and shared across the world. Universities have already gone on-line; so have many schools.

No developmental area has greater effect and few are less contentious, because knowledge is not a zero-sum good. I do not lose knowledge by giving it to others. The reverse is more likely to be the case. It was, for example, the pooling of knowledge, made possible by the invention of printing, the birth of learned societies and the spread of scholarly periodicals, that led to the exponential growth of science in Europe in the seventeenth and eighteenth centuries. More recently it has been the exchange of ideas and discoveries in coffee bars that has made Silicon Valley in California the world leader in computer technologies. Knowledge grows by being shared.

Information technology has not only transformational possibilities but also deep ethical implications. Worldwide, the number of children – girls especially – who lack adequate education is a scandal. It means that most will remain disadvantaged throughout their lives. Schools, curricula, the training of teachers, the provision of computers, and low cost downloading of information should be key forms of international aid and voluntary assistance to developing countries. No other single intervention offers greater prospects of enhancing economic opportunities for everyone, and for moving us forward in the long, hard journey to universal human dignity.

NOTES

1. See Hill 1994; Wright 2000, pp. 174–94.
2. Hill 1994, pp. 12–16.
3. Anderson 1991.
4. Diringer 1962.
5. Ong 1992, p. 85.
6. Ibid., pp. 78–116.
7. See Diringer 1958; Man 2001.
8. Voegelin 1956.
9. *Troilus and Cressida*, Act I, scene iii.
10. See Hillers 1969; Elazar 1995 and 1998.
11. Gottwald 1980, pp. 692—3.
12. Harrison and Huntington 2000, pp. xviii-xix.
13. Nye 2002.
14. Klein 2001.
15. Josephus, *Contra Apionem*, pp. ii, 177–8.
16. Wells, Vol. 1, p. 176.
17. Baron 1945, Vol. 2, p. 172.
18. Soros 2002, pp. 37, 84; Clinton 2001.
19. UN General Assembly, 10 May 2002.

Chapter 8

Co-operation: Civil Society
and its Institutions

Traditional relationships are born of such things as kinship,
ethnicity, geography, and shared spiritual visions. They are
glued together by notions of reciprocal obligations and
visions of common destinies ... Commodified relationships,
on the other hand, are instrumental in nature. The only
glue that holds them together is the agreed-upon transaction
price ... A strong community is a prerequisite for a healthy
economy because it alone produces social trust.

(Jeremy Rifkin, *The Age of Access*)

Enthusiasts of the global market are the latest in the line of those
who been held captive by possibly the single most influential idea
of modernity: that competition is the driving force of progress. In
The Leviathan, Hobbes spoke of the 'general inclination of all
mankind', namely 'a perpetual and restless desire of Power after
power, that ceaseth only in Death'.[1] Charles Darwin, in *The
Origin of Species*, argued that it was the struggle for survival in the
face of finite resources – natural selection – that explained the
course of evolution. Social Darwinians, among them Herbert
Spencer, maintained that the same law of survival applied to
societies and cultures. Today globalists argue that the maximization of competition through financial deregulation and worldwide
markets is the turbo-charged motor of wealth creation.

There is some truth to this proposition, but only some. Understanding how it came to be believed and how more recently it has been challenged, is one of the most enthralling chapters in modern thought, bringing together as it does, converging lines of argument from economics, politics, applied mathematics, sociobiology and computer simulation. The result has been a paradigm shift in our understanding of human interaction, and more importantly a richer sense of the importance of culture and community – what I will call 'covenantal relationships' – in sustaining social life. One of the more significant conclusions is that economics and politics, the two master disciplines of contemporary society, turn out to be insufficient if we are to preserve our human ecology. First, though, how did competition come to occupy centre-stage in modern thought?

One of the turning points in the history of the West came when a series of thinkers asked the question: How can the destructive passions to which human beings are prone be turned to collective advantage? What happens when the sense of sin and the deeply internalized constraints of a religious age, begin to weaken? One answer, given by Hobbes, lay in the creation of a powerful centralized authority, the Leviathan of the state, which would ensure the rule of law. That was the birth of modern politics. The other, perceived by Pascal and Bernard Mandeville among others, was more intriguing. Might not the conflicting desires of individuals be a source of striving, and might this not lead to outcomes better than if human beings were quiescent or even benign? Montesquieu argued that the pursuit of honour energized the body politic, so that 'everyone contributes to the general welfare while thinking that he works for his own interests'. In a similar vein, Giambattista Vico noted that

> Out of ferocity, avarice, and ambition, the three vices which lead all mankind astray, [society] makes national defence, commerce, and politics, and thereby causes the strength, the wealth and the wisdom of the republics; out of these three great vices which would certainly destroy man on earth, society thus causes civil happiness to emerge.

Private vice would become public virtue when society was so organized as to turn passions into interests.[2] Thus was economics born.

The most famous of all articulations of this principle was given, of course, by Adam Smith in *The Wealth of Nations*. Market exchange and the division of labour, he showed, had the effect of creating economic growth. The mysterious but benign nature of this process was that though individuals were driven by self-interest, the aggregate effect was collective gain. Vico, who had already understood this, was moved to say that it 'proves the existence of divine providence'. Smith, more modestly, spoke of 'an invisible hand':

> [The individual] neither intends to promote the public interest, nor knows how much he is promoting it. By preferring the support of domestic to that of foreign industry, he intends only his own security; and by directing that industry in such a manner as its produce may be of the greatest value, he intends only his own gain, and he is in this, as in many other cases, led by an invisible hand to promote an end which was no part of his intention ... By pursuing his own interest he frequently promotes that of the society more effectually than when he really intends to promote it. I have never known much good done by those who affected to trade for the public good. It is an affectation, indeed, not very common among merchants, and very few words need be employed in dissuading them from it.[3]

In a single dazzling insight, this idea resolved one of the great tensions of any culture, between self-interest and altruism, the pursuit of individual and collective gain. There is, it transpires, no conflict after all. The one leads to the other. The power of the market is that it harnesses private energies and turns them to public benefit. Like divine providence itself, it points to a larger pattern in events beyond the intentions of individual agents. Out of the seemingly disconnected decisions of millions of people, each pursuing his or her own advantage, something vast, benign and unexpected emerges: economic growth. To promote the gain of all, all we have to do is concentrate on ourselves. The 'invisible hand' does the rest. This, the central dogma of market economics, was later disputed by the great political alternatives of the modern world, socialism and communism, but by the end of the twentieth century they were already in retreat, even defeat. While democratic capitalism was winning its battle against rival economic systems, though, another challenge was taking shape from a quite different, unexpected direction.[4]

* * *

It began in 1944 with the invention of a new branch of mathematics, games theory, devised by one of the twentieth century's most formidable intelligences: John von Neumann (1903–57). Born in Hungary, the son of a successful banker, he went to the United States in 1930, where he played a leading part in the development of thermonuclear weapons, ballistic missiles and the theory of nuclear deterrence. One particular memory, though, stayed with him from childhood: the conversations his father held around the dinner table about the problems of running a bank. In time this led von Neumann to conclude that economic analysis failed to do justice to a central feature of human decision-making. It is one thing to choose the best of several alternatives when the consequences can be calculated, but life is rarely that simple. Usually the outcome of my choice depends on the reactions of others, and these cannot be predicted. Games theory was an attempt to produce a mathematical representation of action under conditions of uncertainty. Six years later, it yielded its most famous application, the Prisoner's Dilemma.

The dilemma imagines the following scenario. Police arrest two men on suspicion of a serious crime. They lack, however, the evidence to convict. At most, they have enough information to prove them guilty of a lesser offence. The aim of the police, therefore, is to get at least one to inform on the other. They put them in separate rooms with no possibility of communication. They then offer each of the suspects a deal. If one informs and the other stays silent, the informant will go free and the other will receive a jail sentence of ten years. If they both inform on one another, each will receive five years. If they both stay silent, they will be found guilty only of the lesser offence, and each will face a year in prison.

It does not take long to work out that for each, the optimal decision is to inform. The result, though, is that each receives a five-year jail sentence, whereas if they had both stayed silent they would only have been imprisoned for a year. The reason that neither opts for this strategy is that they cannot be sure that the other will do likewise. The Prisoner's Dilemma looks like a mathematical curiosity, but it is far more significant than that. What it does is to challenge the central premiss of Smithian economics, namely that several people, each pursuing their own self-interest, generate an outcome which is beneficial to all. It shows, to the contrary, that two people, both acting rationally, produce a result that is bad for both of them.

For many years this remained a paradox, until insight came from another direction. There had long been a tension in Darwinian biology, of which Charles Darwin was himself aware. In the struggle for survival, the fittest wins. Despite this, almost all human societies value altruistic behaviour and hold it out for emulation. What evolutionary advantage could possibly flow from the sacrifice of one's own interest to that of the group? The group might benefit, but the individual would not. How then would his genes flourish into future generations? As Darwin noted, the bravest individuals 'would on an average perish in larger number than other men'. The hero 'would often leave no offspring to inherit his noble nature'.[5] Altruism should not survive, yet it does.

The answer eventually came through reflection on the Prisoner's Dilemma, which showed that self-interested action did not always yield optimal outcomes. What if the paradox was due to the fact that the parties met only once? What if they met repeatedly? Might they not eventually work out that there was a better strategy, namely co-operation: 'I will stay silent if you do'? I would then be acting in your interest because it was in my interest to do so. This pattern, though, would only emerge once I had a chance to learn; if, in other words, I found myself repeatedly in the same situation, the so-called Iterated Prisoner's Dilemma. This might then solve a problem not only in economics but also in biology. It would explain the origins of altruism.

By the late 1970s the power of computers was great enough to simulate such encounters. A political scientist, Robert Axelrod, announced an international competition to find the program that did best at playing the Iterated Prisoner's Dilemma against itself and other opponents. The winner was devised by a Canadian, Anatole Rapoport, and called Tit-for-Tat. Its procedure was dazzlingly simple: it began by co-operating, and then repeated the last move of its opponent. It worked on the principle, 'What you did to me, I will do to you', or what the Bible and Shakespeare call 'measure for measure'. The more aggressive programs did well in the short run but lost out in the end by provoking retaliation. What Tit-for-Tat showed was the survival value of reciprocal altruism, and thus the evolutionary advantage of *homo sapiens*.

Survival turns out to depend not so much on individual strength as on habits of co-operation. One man loses against a lion, but ten men stand a good chance of winning if they can co-ordinate their efforts. It now seems likely that the distinctive features of human beings – the 300 per cent increase in brain size since our species split from the other primates, and the development of the use of language – derive from the advantages of extended sociality. There is even a close correlation amongst mammals between brain size and social group: the bigger the brain, the larger the group. Interestingly, this measure suggests that the optimum size of a human group is about 150.[6] That, on average, is the maximum number of people we can know well and count as friends. Here is a tantalizing hint that community, that social construct, has a biological base.

Returning, now, to Adam Smith's principle of self-interest, we recall that it seemed to be contradicted by the Prisoner's Dilemma, which showed that self-regarding action often failed to produce optimal outcomes. The conflict was resolved when the game was played many times by the same participants. Eventually they learn to co-operate; and co-operation is predicated on trust, the belief that you will reciprocate, now or later, the actions I take that benefit you. So fundamental is this principle that economists have given it a name. They call it *social capital*, meaning the level of trust in a society. What is crucial, though, is to remember how trust is created through the Iterated Prisoner's Dilemma – namely, by people repeatedly interacting with one another. That, for example, is why crime rates are always higher in inner cities than in villages. Someone is more likely to take advantage of you if you are never going to see him again (the single Prisoner's Dilemma) than if you are going to meet him in the street tomorrow and the day after. Habits of co-operation depend on the existence of long-term relationships.

* * *

How or where, though, does trust begin? There is a paradox here. If it is rational, as the Prisoner's Dilemma shows, not to trust a stranger, where does the breakthrough come? The answer lies in reflecting on the institutions that govern our collective life.

Imagine that you are trying to explain to someone the basic institutions of society. You decide to do so by taking a walk through the centre of London. You pass the Houses of Parliament, and you say that these buildings are the seat of government, the home of politics, and that politics is about the creation and distribution of power. You enter the city proper, passing streets of offices and shops, and seeing in the distance the Stock Exchange building. You say that these are the homes of the market, the domain of economics, and that economics is about the creation and distribution of wealth. As you are walking, your companion points to the steeples and spires of London's churches and the great dome of St Paul's Cathedral. 'And what', she asks, 'do houses of worship create and distribute?' You might be inclined to say that they are not that sort of thing at all, but you would be wrong. Houses of worship, congregations and communities do create and distribute something, but it is significantly different from wealth or power.

Political and economic relationships are *contractual*. They presuppose the coming together of self-interested parties, both of whom benefit from the exchange. In the case of economics, that is self-evident. In the case of politics, it turns on what Hobbes, Locke and Rousseau in their various ways described as the social contract – that process, explicit or implied, whereby individuals give up certain of their powers and freedoms to a central body, the state, which in return undertakes to secure the rule of law and thus the security of life and personal property.

Contractual relationships, however, are not the only or even the most fundamental forms of association. Consider, for example, the family: father, mother and children. They eat, drink, play and occasionally argue together. They take turns to do various chores. They have developed an unconscious choreography of mutuality. They help one another; they depend on one another; and that minuet of giving and taking is a not unimportant part of their identity and growth as individuals. They may have rules, which sometimes get broken. There are minor rebellions which are usually followed by rituals of reconciliation – someone says 'sorry', he or she is forgiven, and order is restored. Watching this microcosm of community and its everyday transactions, we see something significant taking place: the making and sustaining of the moral life.

Beneath the surface of this family are certain fundamental concepts: love, loyalty, responsibility, authority, obedience, fairness and compassion. These are the filaments that hold the family members together. They define their relationships and frame their expectations – that when mother has had a particularly distressing day at work, the others will be a little more sympathetic and less demanding than usual, or that when a younger child finds homework difficult, one of the older ones will help. These relationships are not contractual. They have nothing intrinsically to do with transactions of power or wealth. A group in which getting along together was achieved only by the threat of violence on the one hand, or by paying for services rendered and received on the other, would not be a *family*. I call such relationships – using a keyword of the Bible – *covenantal*. Whereas contracts are about the self, covenants are about the larger groupings in and through which we develop our identity. They are about the 'We' in which I discover the 'I'. Covenantal relationships are those sustained by trust.[7]

One of the governing presuppositions of modern thought was the concept of the isolated or atomic self, the 'I' with which thought and action supposedly began. Descartes famously began his philosophical journey by casting systematic doubt on everything he believed. Of what, if anything, he asked, can I be certain? Of one thing only: I think, therefore I am. This lonely self, assured of nothing save its own existence, is the hero of almost all the great Enlightenment dramas. It is this 'I' which, according to Hobbes, secures its own safety by granting powers to a sovereign. It is the same self which, according to Locke, experiences sensations and uses its powers of reason to develop language. We have already met this 'I' in Adam Smith's story of the market, pursuing its self-interest and thus unwittingly contributing to the wealth of the nation. Selves make contracts.

One of the great intellectual discoveries of the twentieth century, however, is that this 'I' is a fiction, or at the very least an abstraction. The sociologist George Herbert Mead showed that we develop a sense of personal identity only through close and continuous conversation with 'significant others', usually, in the first instance, parents. The philosopher Ludwig Wittgenstein demonstrated that the idea of a 'private language' is incoherent. We learn language only by communicating, by engaging, that is to say, in relationship with others. The Hebrew Bible makes the same point early on – though in a way systematically missed in translation. God says about the first human, 'It is not good for man to be alone.' He then creates the first woman, and the man, waking and seeing her, says: 'This is now bone of my bone, flesh of my flesh; she shall be called woman [*ishah*] because she was taken from man [*ish*].' What is lost in translation is that biblical Hebrew has two words for man, *adam* and *ish*. *Adam* (meaning, taken from the earth, *adamah*) signifies man, the biological species. *Ish* means roughly the same as the English word, 'person'. The subtle point of the biblical text is that this verse is the first in which the word *ish* appears. Adam must pronounce the name of his wife before he can pronounce his own. He must say 'Thou' before he can say 'I'.

It is this conception of personal identity that lies behind the concept of covenant. Covenant is a bond, not of interest or advantage, but of belonging. Covenants are made when two or more people come together to create a 'We'. They differ from contracts in that they tend to be open-ended and enduring. They involve a commitment of the person to another, or to several others. They involve a substantive notion of loyalty – of staying together even in difficult times. They may call, at times, for self-sacrifice. People bound by a covenant are 'obligated to respond to one another beyond the letter of the law rather than to limit their obligations to the narrowest contractual requirements'.[8] The simplest example of a covenant is a marriage. Another is the bond of friendship, as when the Book of Samuel says that 'And Jonathan made a covenant with David because he loved him as himself' (I Samuel 18: 3). But covenants can, and often do, define larger unions. As Daniel Elazar notes, they express 'the idea that people can freely create communities and polities, peoples and publics, and civil society itself through such morally grounded and sustained compacts'.[9]

Covenantal relationships – where we develop the grammar and syntax of reciprocity, where we help others and they help us without calculations of relative advantage – are where trust is born, and without them there would be no selves and no contracts. Contracts, social or economic, mediate relationships between strangers. But if we were always and only strangers to one another, we would have no reason to trust one another. The possibility would always exist, and always have to be taken into consideration, that the other will defect when it is in his or her interest to do so. A world systematically bereft of fidelity or loyalty would be one in which neither states nor markets would ever get under way. Francis Fukuyama is therefore correct when he observes:

> If the institutions of democracy and capitalism are to work properly, they must coexist with certain premodern cultural habits that ensure their proper functioning. Law, contract,

and economic rationality provide a necessary but not sufficient basis for both the stability and prosperity of postindustrial societies; they must as well be leavened with reciprocity, moral obligation, duty toward community, and trust, which are based in habit rather than rational calculation. The latter are not anachronisms in a modern society but rather the sine qua non of the latter's success.[10]

Or, to put it another way: markets depend on virtues not produced by the market, just as states depend on virtues not created by the state.

Where are they created? In families, communities, friendships, congregations, voluntary associations and fellowships of various kinds – in short, wherever people are brought together not by exchange of wealth or power but by commitment to one another or to a larger cause they serve in common. It was this insight that famously led Edmund Burke, reflecting on the French Revolution, to speak of the 'little platoons' as the birthplace of 'public affections'.[11] It was this also that moved Alexis de Tocqueville to assert that it was American 'habits of association' – their tendency to form voluntary associations and join churches – that protected freedom through the exercise of citizenship.[12] Burke and Tocqueville have been subjects of intense interest in recent years because of a growing realization that between them, the market and the state have weakened trust-creating institutions – sometimes called 'third-sector' or 'mediating' structures. Those who seek to reinvigorate them are sometimes called 'communitarians'. Others prefer the term 'civil society'.[13] Yet others, as mentioned above, speak of social capital. What they have in common is their emphasis on non-contractual, or what I have called covenantal relationships. Without them, not only do markets and states begin to falter. Social life itself loses grace and civility. The bonds that connect us to one another start to fray. The sense of identity and belonging become ever more tenuous. We begin to feel vulnerable and alone. We can now say what houses of worship and their attendant communities once created and is now in danger of being lost – that covenantal dimension of life that generates trust.

It was Harvard political scientist Robert Putnam who in 1995 gave the phenomenon a metaphor and name. Noting that more Americans were going ten-pin bowling than before, but fewer were joining leagues, he called it 'bowling alone'.[14] His argument was that social capital was in decline throughout the liberal democracies of the West. This could be seen not only in the breakdown of families and communities, but across the whole range of civic and social engagements. Fewer people were joining voluntary groups. Church attendance was down. People spent less time with their neighbours. The young were markedly less interested than their parents in politics. 'Habits of association' were being lost, and the consequence was inevitable. The Iterated Prisoner's Dilemma implies that repeated interaction with a stable group of others is essential to the maintenance of trust. When a society loses these contexts, individuals become more guarded and suspicious. They feel themselves surrounded by strangers, not friends. Putnam and others measured this loss. They found that people were more suspicious about the motives of others and more cynical about politicians. There was a generalized loss of confidence in authorities and institutions.

The irony is that Adam Smith seems to have known this all along, for he wrote not one masterpiece but two: not only *The Wealth of Nations* (1776) but also, and first, *The Theory of Moral Sentiments* (1759). In that earlier work, far from championing self-interest, he wrote that 'to feel much for others, and little for us ... constitutes the perfection of human nature'. German scholars, puzzled by the apparent contradiction between the two books, called it *das Adam Smith Problem*. The resolution, though, should by now be clear. There is an economic system and a moral one. The first belongs to the market, the second to the concentric circles of family, friends, community and society. When the moral system encompasses the economic one, it produces the virtues of industry, honesty and mutual reliability on which the market depends. It is when the economic system subverts the moral one that trust is endangered and we move toward the situation of the initial Prisoner's Dilemma, in which the pursuit of self-interest is harmful rather than beneficial. The paradox of competition is that it is benign only when counterbalanced by habits of co-operation. A purely competitive world begins by being creative but ends by becoming self-destructive.

* * *

The new economy has an adverse effect on trust, and it does so in multiple ways. One is what Robert Reich strikingly calls 'the obsolescence of loyalty'.[15] The sheer pressure of change means that jobs are no longer secure. Companies are constantly 'downsizing', 'deselecting' or 're-engineering', shedding employees or putting them on part-time or project-specific contracts. Companies that used to pride themselves on lifetime commitment to their workers have been forced to abandon the policy and announce large job losses. Large corporations that once dominated particular towns, employing a significant part of their workforce, now outsource much of their production abroad and have ceased to be major civic presences. Whole areas of employment can, it seems, be wiped out almost overnight. *Encyclopaedia Britannica*, a 230-year-old company, disbanded its entire door-to-door sales force when it went online. In a business environment in which there is constant pressure on employers, employees, consumers and investors to switch to something better ever more rapidly, notes Reich, 'enterprises are becoming collections of people bound to one another by little more than temporary convenience'.[16] It is hard to know who owes loyalty to whom, or whether the word has any relevance at all in the contemporary world.

In *The Crisis of Global Capitalism*, George Soros notes that when he began his career in the 1950s, business depended on the slow building of relationships. Now it has become 'transactional', a series of one-off encounters, contract by contract, deal by deal, which depend not on trust but on the presence of lawyers:

> In a perfectly changeable, transactional society the individual is paramount. From the point of view of the individual it is not necessary to be morally upright to be successful; indeed it can be a hindrance ... In a society where stable relationships prevail, this is much less of a problem because

it is difficult to be successful if you violate the prevailing social norms. But when you can move around freely, social norms become less binding, and when expediency becomes established as the social norm, society becomes unstable.[17]

The loss of loyalty extends into private life as well. There are many reasons for the extraordinary breakdown of the family that has occurred throughout the West since the 1960s. One, though, surely is intrusion of market values into areas that had previously been immune. A consumer-driven, advertising-dominated culture militates daily against ongoing attachments. It is constantly inviting us to switch to a different brand, try something new, go for a better deal elsewhere. It should not come as a surprise that this begins to affect human relationships as well. A society saturated by market values would be one in which relationships were temporary, loyalties provisional and commitments easily discarded. It would, in short, be one in which marriage made little sense – and that, by and large, is what has happened.

Time itself, in the new economy, works against the institutions of civil society. When people are forced, as they are now, to work harder and be constantly on call by fax, cell phone, voice-mail and e-mail, time that used to be spent on family, friends and voluntary work is no longer there. It is not just that work has become more demanding, and involves more travel and more frequent relocation. Its very insecurity forces people to work harder in case, next month or next year, they no longer have a job, at least one that pays as well. The result is that people, at least during their working lives, have less free time to spend on non-economic activity. Work that used to be done within the family, from child-care to preparing food, is increasingly being done by someone else for pay. The family is becoming downsized and outsourced. Parents spend less time with their children, who in turn spend more time watching television or glued to the computer screen. The result is, as Jeremy Rifkin puts it:

[W]hen most relationships become commercial relationships and every individual's life is commodified twenty-four hours a day, what is left for relationships of a non-commercial nature – relationships based on kinship, neighbourliness, shared cultural interests, religious affiliation, ethnic identi-fication, and fraternal or civic involvement? When time itself is bought and sold and one's life becomes little more than an ongoing series of commercial transactions held together by contracts and financial instruments, what happens to the kind of traditional reciprocal relationships that are born of affection, love, and devotion?[18]

Not only time, but place too, becomes commercialized. Civil society depends on environments where people meet, mix and form attachments that cut across barriers of class or ethnicity. That was one of the historic roles of places of worship, but in other and different ways it is the role of public spaces in general – parks, squares, mixed neighbourhoods, the places you go where you do not have to pay. There are fewer and fewer such environments. Communities become more segregated as the rich move else-where. Parks become more dangerous as street crime rises. The great public arenas have become shopping malls and entertain-ment complexes, but these are not civic spaces. We go there as consumers, not as fellow citizens. More and more of our encounters are disembodied. We communicate increasingly by phone and e-mail, less by personal presence. The result is a loss of human contact and all that implies. Virtual communities are no substitute for the real thing. John Gray spells out the danger:

> The mirage of virtual community serves to reconcile us to the growing dereliction of the social institutions and public places in which ... unprogrammed encounters occur. If cities are desolated and schools stalked by fear, if we shrink from strangers and children as threats to our safety, a retreat into the empty freedom of cyberspace may seem like a liberation. Yet living much of our lives in this space means giving up part of what makes us human.[19]

* * *

These things matter, and I have tried in this chapter to say why. Sociologists speak about trust, economists about social capital, sociobiologists about reciprocal altruism, political theorists about civil society. What these various terms signify is that social life cannot be reduced to a series of market exchanges. We need covenants as well as contracts; meanings as well as preferences; loyalties, not just temporary associations for mutual gain. These things go to the heart of who we are. They are the 'signals of transcendence' in the midst of fast-paced world.

For life to have personal meaning, there must be people who matter to us, and for whom we matter, unconditionally and non-substitutably. Ask someone what his or her greatest source of happiness is, and they are unlikely to mention their latest car, their last holiday, their new designer jeans. They are, or were, more likely to say: my marriage partner, my children, my reputation, my friends. Lose these and we lose the very concept of happiness, of a life well lived, of dedication to something larger than ourselves. Measurably, that is what has happened. In a single generation, despite economic progress and technological advance, the incidence of depressive illness, stress-related syndromes, suicide attempts and alcohol and drug abuse have all risen. These are not symptoms of well-being, and they remind us of what so much in today's world seeks to make us forget: that we were not made to serve economic systems. They were made to serve us.

The consumerization of society has left us freer to choose almost everything: what to do, where to go, how to live and with whom. But that freedom simultaneously dissolves the very things that once gave permanence and dignity to a life. Marriages become fragile. Attendance at places of worship declines. Voluntary groups are more fragmented and ephemeral. It becomes hard for individuals to find stable networks of support at the very time they need them most. It becomes even harder to say why we do what we do. Politicians value us for our vote, advertisers for what we buy, but who is left to value us for what we are? When contracts displace covenants and means replace ends, we are left with freedom without meaning, which is certainly more pleasant but not necessarily more fulfilling than meaning without freedom.

To be sure, the problem does not arise in the same way throughout the world. In some societies, most notably the liberal democracies of the West, individualism may have gone too far. In others – those that have not yet, or only recently, become democratized – it may not have gone far enough. Excessive centralization inhibits the growth of civil associations, just as excessive commercialization erodes them.[20] The proper balance is precarious and hard to maintain. Yet the encouragement of civil society is an essential feature of the successful transition from totalitarian societies and centralized economies to democratic capitalism, just as it is a necessary element of liberal democracy itself. Without stable association with others over extended periods of time, we fail to acquire the habits of co-operation which form the basis of trust on which the economics and politics of a free society depend.

One of the classic roles of religion has been to preserve a space – physical and metaphysical – immune to the pressures of the market. When we stand before God we do so regardless of what we earn, what we own, what we buy, what we can afford. We do so as beings of ultimate, non-transactional value, here because someone – some force at the heart of being – called us into existence and summoned us to be a blessing. The power of the great world religions is that they are not mere philosophical systems, abstract truths strung together in strictly logical configurations. They are embodied truths, made vividly real in lives, homes, congregations, rituals, narratives, songs and prayers – in covenantal communities whose power is precisely that they are not subject to economic forces. They value people for what they are; they value actions for the ideals that brought them forth; they preserve relationships by endowing them with the charisma of eternity made real in the here-and-now. As Roger Scruton puts it:

> Faith exalts the human heart, by removing it from the market-place, making it sacred and unexchangeable. Under the jurisdiction of religion our deeper feelings are sacralized, so as to become raw material for the ethical life: the life lived

in judgement. When faith declines, however, the sacred is unprotected from marauders; the heart can be captured and put on sale.[21]

There have been, and still are, religions opposed in principle to the market. Judaism, as I have tried to make clear, is not one of them. It values the free economy because it values freedom; because it leads to creativity and the progressive liberation of human lives from the random cruelties of nature – poverty, famine, drudgery and disease. The world we have made is better than our ancestors knew. We live longer, we travel further, we spend less time in pure routine. There is nothing in Judaism of nostalgia for the golden age, the mythical past, paradise lost, a remembered Eden. But even a faith as focused on this world as Judaism, insists on limits. There are times and places – the Sabbath, festivals, daily prayer, the home, the school, the house of study – into which the market and its siren voices may not intrude. What George Soros calls 'market fundamentalism' is a form of idolatry – taking a man-made artefact and endowing it with transcendental value. The market is a means, not an end.

I am encouraged that the World Bank, under James Wolfensohn, has begun a dialogue with religious leaders, with a view to directing economic development in ways that respect and try to preserve local communities, their traditions and institutions. I have shown that this is not just important from the point of view of human dignity. It is also sound economics. It is not enough to build factories, transportation systems and computer networks if in the process one destroys communities and the subtle ties that bind people to one another. If co-operation without competition is lame, then competition without co-operation is blind. The people who make and buy, work and consume, are *people*, and creating an environment that respects people and the relationships they need to sustain respect, is an essential part of what Samuel Brittan calls 'capitalism with a human face'.[22]

NOTES

1. Hobbes 1991, p. 70.
2. Hirschman 1997.
3. Smith 1937, p. 423.
4. The story is told best in Wright 1995; Ridley 1996; and Fukuyama 1999.
5. Charles Darwin, *The Descent of Man*, Vol. 1, p. 163.
6. Gladwell 2001, pp. 169–92.
7. On trust, see Fukuyama 1995; Seligman 1997.
8. Elazar 1989, p. 19.
9. Ibid.
10. Fukuyama 1995, p. 11.
11. Burke 1993, p. 198.
12. Tocqueville 1968.
13. On communitarianism and civil society, see Sacks 2000 and the literature cited there. See also Dionne 1998; Eberly 1995 and 2000; Glendon and Blankenhorn 1995; Warren 1999 and 2001.
14. Robert Putnam, 'Bowling Alone: America's Declining Social Capital', *Journal of Democracy* (January 1995): pp. 65–78.
15. Reich 2001, pp. 65–83.
16. Ibid., p. 83.
17. Soros 1998, p. 80.
18. Rifkin 2000, p. 112.
19. Gray 1997, p. 120.
20. Soros 2000.
21. Scruton 1998, p. 84.
22. Brittan 1995.

Chapter 9

Conservation: Environmental Sustainability

> I believe that we have little chance of averting an environmental catastrophe unless we recognize that we are not the masters of Being, but only a part of Being ... We must recognize that we are related to more than to the present moment and the present place, that we are related to the world as a whole and to eternity. We must recognize that, by failing to reflect universal, supra-individual and supra-temporal interests, we do a disservice to our specific, local and immediate interests. Only people with a sense of responsibility for the world and to the world are truly responsible to and for themselves.
>
> (Václav Havel, *The Art of the Impossible*)

The giant stone statues of Easter Island are an eerie reminder of the human capacity to destroy the ecological resources we need in order to survive. Easter Island, in the Pacific Ocean, 2,300 miles west of Chile, is one of the remotest places on earth. When the Dutch explorer Jakob Roggeveen came there in 1722 he found almost a thousand of the statues, some weighing to 85 tons and up to 37 feet tall. Hewn from volcanic quarries, over 300 statues had been transported miles and raised upright on platforms by the island inhabitants, despite the fact that they had no metal or wheels or any power source other than their own energy. Hundreds more lay unfinished in the quarries or abandoned before reaching their destination. The whole scene was a mystery, unfathomed until recently.

Thor Heyerdal and others in the twentieth century gradually pieced together the story of what had happened. When Polynesians settled the island in the fourth or fifth century, it was covered by dense forest. Little by little they cut down the trees. Some they used as rollers to transport the statues. Others they removed to create clearings for agriculture and to carve into canoes for fishing. Eventually not a single tree remained. The statues could no longer be moved, and were abandoned. The soil eroded and produced a lower yield of crops. There was no more wood for canoes, so that the islanders caught fewer fish and had less protein in their diet. The economy gradually collapsed. The inhabitants divided into clans and began fighting one another. The landscape became littered with spear points. Rival groups tore down one another's statues. People captured in battle were either eaten or enslaved. The island which had once supported 7,000 people was reduced to a third of its former population, many of them living in caves for protection. Easter Island is a forewarning of what may happen to the planet as a whole if we continue to consume resources and destroy habitats at our present rate.[1]

The record of human intervention in the natural order is marked by devastation on a massive scale. Within a thousand years, the first human inhabitants of America had travelled from the Arctic north to the southernmost tip of Patagonia, making their way through two continents and, on the way, destroying most of the large mammal species then extant, among them mammoths, mastodons, tapirs, camels, horses, lions, cheetahs and bears. When the first British colonists arrived in New Zealand in the early nineteenth century, bats were the only native land mammals they found. They discovered, however, traces of a large ostrich-like bird the Maoris called 'moa'. Eventually skeletons of a dozen species of this animal came to light ranging from three to ten feet high. The remains of some 28 other species have been found, among them flightless ducks, coots and geese, together with pelicans, swans, ravens and eagles. Animals that have not had to face human predators before are easy game, and the Maoris must have found them a relatively effortless source of food. A similar pattern can be traced almost everywhere human beings have set foot.

What has changed, of course, is the pace and scope of environmental devastation that has followed in the wake of industrialization, pollution and the destruction of rain forests. Today, 1,666 of the 9,000 bird species are endangered or at imminent risk of extinction. If present trends continue, half of the world's total of 30 million animal and plant species will become extinct in the course of the next century. Partly this has been caused by excessive hunting, for example of African elephants and rhinos for their tusks and horns. In part it has been caused by the introduction of new species to a particular area that kill or infect existing animals, or by the transfer of the pests like the fungi which carried Dutch elm disease. The destruction of habitats, such as the draining of marshland, disturbs the ecological balance on which many life forms depend. Ecuador, Madagascar and the Philippines have already lost at least two-thirds of their rain forests which are some of the richest of all homes of animal and plant life. Most significant of all is the pressure on the environment by the growth of the human population, which has increased from half a billion in 1600 to six billion today, and continues to rise. Biologist E. O. Wilson is blunt in his prognosis:

> The ongoing loss of biodiversity is the greatest since the end of the Mesozoic Era sixty-five million years ago. At that time, by current scientific consensus, the impact of one or more giant meteorites darkened the atmosphere, altered much of Earth's climate, and extinguished the dinosaurs. Thus began the next stage of evolution, the Cenozoic Era or Age of Mammals. The extinction spasm we are now inflicting can be moderated if we so choose. Otherwise, the next century will see the closing of the Cenozoic Era and a new one characterized not by new life forms but by biological impoverishment. It might appropriately be called the 'Eremozoic Era', the Age of Loneliness.[2]

*   *   *

In no other sphere of current concern has there been a more religious tone to public awareness. Rightly so, for it is here if anywhere that we come face to face with the fundamental questions of our place in the universe and our responsibility for it: with the destructive potential of human intervention on the one hand, and on the other the awe-inspiring beauty of so many of the life forms now at risk. Ancient pagan ideas have been revived, among them James Lovelock's 'Gaia' hypothesis that the earth is a single organism (Gaia was the Greek earth goddess, a name suggested to Lovelock by the novelist William Golding).[3] It is not clear, though, that earth worship is the best way of charting a path forward. Earth worshippers were as destructive of life forms as any other group, and as philosopher John Passmore points out,[4] the cure may be worse than the disease. To turn our back on technology will not improve but substantially reduce human welfare, now and in the future. More significantly, it will impair our ability to conserve nature as well as exploit it. What is needed is not less science but a more far-sighted view of its effects.

Passmore's own view is that the Hebrew Bible is a key source of ecological awareness. Few passages have had a deeper influence on Western civilization than the first chapter of Genesis with its momentous vision of the universe coming into being as the work of God. Mankind, the last and greatest of creations, is given dominion over nature: 'Be fruitful and multiply, fill the earth and subdue it.' There is a sense of wonder here, and more explicitly in Psalm 8, at the smallness yet uniqueness of mankind, vulnerable but also unique in his ability to shape the environment:

> When I consider your heavens,
> The work of your fingers,
> The moon and the stars,
> Which you have set in place.
> What is man that you are mindful of him,
> The son of man that you care for him?
> Yet you have made him little lower than the angels
> And crowned him with glory and honour. (Psalm 8: 3–5)

It was Max Weber, the nineteenth-century sociologist, who argued that it was here that lay the roots of Western rationalism and the 'disenchantment' or demythologization of nature. For the first time God was not identified with the forces of nature but set entirely beyond them. The universe was stripped bare of the overlay of myth, no longer the dwelling place of mysterious, capricious and unfathomable gods but an arena in which human beings could act and exercise rational control. Without this 'secularization' of the world, suggested Weber, the scientific enterprise might never have begun.

Genesis 1 is, however, only one side of the complex biblical equation. It is balanced by a narrative, quite different in tone, in Genesis 2, in which the first man is set in the garden of Eden 'to work it and take care of it'. The two Hebrew verbs used here are significant. The first – *le'ovdah* – literally means 'to serve it'. Man is thus both master and servant of nature. The second – *leshomrah* – means 'to guard it'. This is the verb used in later biblical legislation to describe the responsibilities of a guardian of property that does not belong to him. He must exercise vigilance in his protection and is liable for loss through negligence. This is perhaps the best short definition of man's responsibility for nature as the Bible conceives it.

We do not own nature – 'The earth is the Lord's and the fullness thereof.' We are its trustees on behalf of God who made it and owns it, and for the sake of future generations. It was for this reason, incidentally, that in 1995 I joined some 200 other signatories from the world's great faiths in opposing the granting of patents on animal and human genes, organs, tissues and organisms. Life forms are not inventions but discoveries. They do not belong to scientists or biochemical corporations but equally to all and none of us: they are God's loan, entrusted to our collective care.

Not only do we not own nature: we are duty bound to respect its integrity. The mid-nineteenth-century commentator Samson Raphael Hirsch puts this rather well in an original interpretation of the phrase in Genesis 1: 'Let us make man in our image after our own likeness.' The passage has always been puzzling, for at that stage, prior to the creation of man, God was alone. The 'us', says Hirsch, refers to the rest of creation. Because man alone would develop the capacity to change and possibly endanger the natural world, nature itself was consulted as to whether it approved of such a being. The implied condition is that man would use nature only in such a way as to be faithful to the purposes of its creator. The mandate to exercise dominion is therefore not technical but moral and is limited by the requirement to protect and conserve. Indeed, the famous story of Genesis 2–3 – the eating of the forbidden fruit and man's subsequent exile from Eden – seems to make just this point. Not everything is permitted. There are limits to what we may do, and when they are transgressed, disaster follows: 'Dust you are, and to dust you will return' (Genesis 3: 19).

Environmentalists have sometimes claimed that Genesis 1 is the source of the Western disdain for nature, seeing it as Bacon and Descartes did, as inert, malleable and to be shaped to human purposes as we choose. Passmore has so effectively refuted this idea that there is little to add to his comment that 'It is only as a result of Greek influence' that seventeenth-century thinkers and their successors were 'led to think of nature as nothing but a system of resources, man's relationships with which are in no respect subject to moral censure'.[5] In fact, Genesis sets forth a view of nature which is not man-centred but God-centred. To be sure, humanity with its unique capacity for moral choice is the focus of its concerns. But Maimonides warns us against an anthropocentric view of reality. 'The universe does not exist for man's sake, but each being exists for its own sake and not because of some other thing.'[6] That is implicit throughout the prophetic literature and in the great creation psalms:

> You make springs gush forth in the valleys;
> They flow between the hills,
> Giving drink to every wild animal;
> The wild asses quench their thirst.
> By the streams the birds of the air have their habitation;
> They sing among the branches.

From your lofty abode you water the mountains;
The earth is satisfied with the fruit of your work.
You cause the grass to grow fat for the cattle,
And plants for people to use. (Psalm 104: 10–14)

Creation has its own dignity as God's masterpiece, and though we have the mandate to use it, we have none to destroy or despoil it.

* * *

Though we must exercise caution when reading twenty-first century concerns into ancient texts, there seems little doubt that much biblical legislation is concerned with what we would nowadays call 'sustainability'. This is particularly true of the three great commands ordaining periodic rest: the Sabbath, the sabbatical year and the jubilee year. On the Sabbath all agricultural work is forbidden, 'so that your ox and your donkey may rest' (Exodus 23: 12). It is a day that sets a limit to our intervention in nature and the pursuit of economic activity. We become conscious of being creations, not creators. The earth is not ours but God's. For six days it is handed over to us, but on the seventh day we symbolically abdicate that power. We may perform no 'work', which is to say, an act that alters the state of something for human purposes. The Sabbath is a weekly reminder of the integrity of nature and the boundaries of human striving.

What the Sabbath does for human beings and animals, the sabbatical and jubilee years do for the land. The earth too is entitled to its periodic rest. The Bible warns that if the Israelites do not respect this, they will suffer exile: 'Then shall the land make up for its sabbatical years throughout the time that it is desolate and you are in the land of your enemies; then shall the land rest and make up for its sabbath years' (Leviticus 26: 34). Behind this are two concerns. One is environmental. As Maimonides points out, land which is over-exploited is eventually eroded and loses its fertility. The Israelites were therefore commanded to conserve the soil by giving it periodic fallow years and not pursue short-term gain at the cost of long-term desolation. The second, no less significant, is theological: 'The

167

land', says God, 'is Mine; you are but strangers resident with Me' (Leviticus 25: 23). We are guests on earth.

* * *

Another group of commandments is directed against interference with nature. The Bible forbids crossbreeding livestock, planting a field with mixed seeds, and wearing a garment of mixed wool and linen. It calls these rules *chukkim* or 'statutes'. The thirteenth-century scholar Nahmanides understood this term to mean laws which respect the integrity of nature. To mix different species, he argued, was to presume to be able to improve on the order of creation, and thus an affront to the Creator. Each species has its own internal laws of development and reproduction, and these must not be tampered with: 'One who combines two different species thereby changes and defies the work of creation, as if he believes that the Holy One, blessed be He, has not completely perfected the world and he now wishes to improve it by adding new kinds of creatures.' Deuteronomy also contains a law which forbids taking a young bird together with its mother. Nahmanides sees this as having the same underlying concern, namely of protecting species. Though the Bible permits us to use some animals for food, we must not cull them to extinction.

It was, though, Samson Raphael Hirsch in the nineteenth century who gave the most forcible interpretation of biblical law. The statutes relating to environmental protection, he said, represented the principle that 'the same regard which you show to man you must also demonstrate to every lower creature, to the earth which bears and sustains all, and to the world of plants and animals'. They represented a kind of social justice applied to the natural world: 'They ask you to regard all living things as God's property. Destroy none; abuse none; waste nothing; employ all things wisely ... Look upon all creatures as servants in the household of creation.'[7]

At about the same time that Hirsch was writing, a British Jew, Lewis Gompertz (1779–1861) was pioneering the concept of animal rights, a campaign which led to the creation of the organization now known as the Royal Society for the Prevention of Cruelty to Animals (RSPCA). Peter Singer, the philosopher who has done more to argue this case than any other in our time, tells of his surprise when, studying in the British Library, he came across one of Gompertz's works and discovered that he 'had been thinking along similar lines 150 years earlier'. In his essay *Moral Inquiries on the Situation of Man and of Brutes* (1824), Gompertz looked forward to the time when

> man, then becoming truly religious, will glory in super-intending the works of his Maker, which he has entrusted to him: as a faithful servant, he will then not deny to what he now calls the meanest reptile, his protection, and own it to be his brother, resembling himself in construction, and created with similar care by the Supreme Being.[8]

* * *

It is not my aim here to set out in detail Jewish environmental legislation, of which there has been a continuous tradition since biblical times. Not all took the view of Nahmanides and Hirsch that any intervention in the natural order was forbidden. Others believed that creation was left deliberately incomplete so that we, too, could play our part in 'perfecting the world under the sovereignty of God'. For that reason, for example, Jewish law is not opposed to *in vitro* fertilization or, with appropriate safe-guards, stem-cell research. Nature is not sacrosanct. If it were, we would be bound to respect viruses, genetic illness and 'the thousand natural shocks that flesh is heir to'. Some authorities, following Nahmanides, would ban genetically modified crops; others would permit them if their safety were adequately tested and they offered the chance of alleviating hunger and need. All, though, would agree that we are charged with conserving and protecting the world's resources so that future generations would benefit – a point brought out by a simple Talmudic story about one of the saints of early rabbinic times, Honi the Circle-Drawer:

> One day Honi was journeying on the road and saw a man planting a carob tree. He asked him, 'How long does it take

for a carob tree to bear fruit?' The man replied, 'Seventy years.' Honi asked, 'Are you certain that you will live another seventy years?' The man answered, 'I found carob trees in the world. As my forefathers planted them for me, so I too plant these for my children.'[9]

Constructing an environmental ethic in strictly secular terms has proved unexpectedly difficult. On what basis do we owe 'duties to nature', given that nature does not recognize duties to itself or to us, and thus lies outside the domains of contract and reciprocity? In what sense do we owe duties to generations as yet unborn, who are clearly not moral agents since they do not currently exist? On what rational basis are we to factor future loss of biodiversity as against present gain? What calculus would guide governments in poor countries who need the land made available by the clearing of forests to provide fields and food for hungry populations? Given the global impact of local policies, are wealthier nations obligated to compensate others for their environmental self-restraint? And what would persuade the citizens of those wealthy nations to give up resource-consuming habits of consumption? On what logical basis, Hans Jonas asked, do we even have a moral responsibility to ensure that there is a world for future generations to inhabit?[10]

The power of the religious imagination is not that it has easy answers to difficult questions, but that it provides a framework of thought for such large and intractable issues. It is easier to understand the moral constraints on action when we believe that there is someone to whom we owe responsibility, that we are not owners of the planet, and that we are covenantally linked to those who will come after us. Like the planter of the carob tree, we act so that those who come after us will have a world to enjoy as we did. Hilary Putnam points out that no less important to ethics than abstract concepts like rights and duties, is what he calls a 'moral image', a picture that gives shape to the whole.[11] That is what we need now. The simplest image, and surely the most sensible one, in thinking about our ecological responsibilities is to see the earth as belonging to the source of being, and us as its trustees, charged with conserving and if possible beautifying it for the sake of our grandchildren not yet born.

Nor is this all. As I pointed out in an earlier chapter, religions are not philosophical systems. They are embodied truths, made real in the lives of communities. It is one thing to have an abstract conception of ecological responsibility, another to celebrate the Sabbath weekly – to renounce our mastery of nature one day in seven – and to make a blessing, as Jews do, over everything we eat or drink to remind ourselves of God's ownership of the world. Prayer, ritual and narrative are ways we shape what Tocqueville called 'habits of the heart'. They form character, create behavioural dispositions and educate us in patterns of self-restraint. Roger Scruton makes a fascinating observation in relation to BSE or 'mad cow disease' and the biblical prohibition against 'seething a kid in its mother's milk':

> The Jewish law which forbids us to seethe a young animal in its mother's milk may have little sense, when considered from the standpoint of a hard-nosed utilitarianism. But our disposition to hesitate before the mystery of nature, to renounce our presumption of mastery, and to respect the process by which life is made, must surely prompt us to sympathise with such an interdiction. And these very same feelings, had we allowed them to prevail, would have caused us to hesitate before feeding to cows, which live and thrive on pasture, the dead remains of their own and other species.[12]

We will need cultivated instincts of caution if we are to hold ourselves back from patterns of production and consumption that threaten the future of the planet.

All of the world's great faiths embody a sense of respect for nature,[13] and thus constitute an important counterbalance to the indifference bordering on arrogance that has been one of the less lovely legacies of the Enlightenment. One of the defining beliefs of modernity was that science and technology would unlock the bounties of nature and lead to open-ended progress toward unlimited abundance. In the words of Christopher Lasch, 'Progressive optimism rests, at bottom, on a denial of the natural limits on human power and freedom, and it cannot survive for very long in a world in which an awareness of those limits has become inescapable.'[14]

Civilizations at the height of their powers have found it hard to maintain a sense of limits. Each in turn has been captivated by the idea that it alone was immune to the laws of growth and decline, that it could consume resources indefinitely, pursuing present advantage without thought of future depletion. Never is this more likely than when we lose the sense of awe in the face of totality. 'But in proportion as the light of faith grows dim, the range of man's sight is circumscribed', wrote Alexis de Tocqueville. 'When men have once allowed themselves to think no more of what is to befall them after life, they lapse readily into that complete and brutal indifference to futurity which is all but too conformable to some propensities of mankind.'[15] The great faiths teach a different kind of wisdom: *reverence* in the face of creation, *responsibility* to future generations, and *restraint* in the knowledge that not everything we can do, should we do.

Every technological civilization faces two opposing dangers. One is the hubris that says: we have godlike powers, therefore let us take the place of God. The other is the fear that says: in the name of God, let us not use these godlike powers at all. Both are wrong. Each technological advance carries with it the possibility of diminishing or enhancing human dignity. What matters is how we use it. The way to use it is in covenant with God, honouring His image that is mankind. At the end of his book *Consilience*, E. O. Wilson draws this sombre conclusion:

[W]e are learning the fundamental principle that ethics is everything ... We are adults who have discovered which covenants are necessary for our survival, and we have accepted the necessity of securing them by sacred oath ... [I]f we should surrender our genetic nature to machine-aided ratiocination, and our ethics and art and our very meaning to a habit of careless discursion in the name of progress, imagining ourselves to be god-like and absolved from our ancient heritage, we will become nothing.[16]

Or, as an ancient rabbinic comment put it: when God finished creating the universe he said to the first human being: 'Behold my works, how beautiful, how splendid they are. All that I have created, I created for you. Take care, therefore, that you do not destroy my world, for if you do, there will be no one left to repair what you have destroyed.'[17]

*   *   *

The natural environment is both example and metaphor of the theme that has threaded through the various arguments of this book: the dignity of difference – the insistence that what is most precious in our world, and constantly at risk, is diversity itself. In some ways this is a relatively recent discovery. We are more aware than any previous generation of how much our existence depends on the presence of other species, which produce the food we eat and the oxygen we breathe, absorb the carbon dioxide we exhale, sustain the fertility of the soil and provide the raw materials we need. Those species in turn depend on others; and others still may, in ways yet unknown, turn out to contain vitally important antibiotics or other medicinal agents – 40 per cent of all medicines used today depend on substances originally extracted from plants, fungi, animals and micro-organisms. We are beginning to understand how complex and interdependent biosystems are, and how unpredictable the consequences are of the destruction of a species or habitat. Diversity needs protection.

What applies to nature applies to culture. I have argued that the free market exists in virtue of difference. Ricardo's law of comparative advantage tells us that each of us has something to contribute to the collective good, and that we each gain from the distinctive skills and excellences of others. That is true of all trade, and there is therefore every reason to believe that the sheer growth of international trade bought about by globalization is fundamentally benign. No other system has offered more genuine prospects for the alleviation of suffering, poverty, ignorance and disease for more people since civilization began.

In many respects, though, the protestors are right. The distribution of benefits within and between countries leaves large groups permanently excluded, with many of them less well off than they were a generation ago. The destabilizing effects of the modern market and the sheer speed of change have left us all less secure, and that has been combined with an erosion of the social ecology that once provided people with networks of support as well as systems of moral meaning. These are not minor problems. They go to the very heart of the human project: constructing a society of substantive justice, collective grace and equal access to the preconditions of dignity.

I have proposed a simple set of ideas that might guide us in the choppy waters ahead. *Control* means taking responsibility and refusing to see economic or political developments as inevitable. *Contribution* means that there is a moral dimension to economics. Advertisers who mislead, producers who turn a blind eye to inhumane working conditions and starvation wages, beneficiaries of the system who do not share their time or blessings with others, are unacceptable whether or not what they do is legal. *Compassion* means that developing countries must take seriously their obligation to the world's poor, protecting their independence while opening up ways of escaping from poverty. *Creativity* suggests that (not the only, but) the best way of doing this is through investment in education. *Co-operation* tells us that markets do not survive on the basis of competition alone. They presuppose virtues and what I have called covenantal relationships, without which the Prisoner's Dilemma tells us that individual self-interest will fail to generate collective good. *Conservation* reminds us of our duties to nature and to the future, without which the pace of economic growth will merely be a measure of the speed at which we approach the abyss.

This moral framework is not an attempt to minimize the awesome complexity of the decisions governments, corporations and individuals have to take. But complexity can sometimes be an excuse for ignoring the moral dimension; and if we do that, we are lost. Freedom means restraint. It means not doing everything we can do, nor doing something on the grounds that if we do not, someone else will. The free market is a wondrous device, but to suppose that it or any other value-neutral process – the balance of power in international politics, for example, or the development of genetic research – will yield of themselves optimal outcomes is to have the kind of naïve faith that belongs to an older, simpler world. Fundamentalisms, we should never forget, can be economic or scientific as well as religious. Without a moral vision, we will fail. And that vision, to be shared, can only emerge from conversation – from talking to one another and listening to one another across boundaries of class, income, race and faith.

Which brings me back to where I began. The tensions that September 11 exposed have not diminished. The Middle East is at boiling point. Europe has been simmering with religious and ethnic conflict. There has been violence in India, Pakistan, Kashmir. It would be hard to identify any factor that has made prospects for peace anywhere brighter now than they were a year ago. Is there a key to conflict resolution? Is there anything that has the power to generate hope in regions of despair? Can we ever turn enemies into friends?

NOTES

1. See Diamond 1992, pp. 317–62.
2. Wilson 1999, p. 310.
3. Mary Midgley, 'Individualism and the concept of Gaia', in Booth, et al. 2001, pp. 29–44.
4. Passmore 1980.
5. Ibid., p. 27.
6. Maimonides, *Guide for the Perplexed*, 3: 13. On biblical images of nature, see Brown 1999.
7. Hirsch 1969, p. 79.
8. Gompertz 1992, p. 51.
9. Babylonian Talmud, *Taanit*, p. 23a.
10. Jonas 1984.
11. Hilary Putnam, 'Cloning People', in Burley 1999, pp. 1–13.

that event. It had been a recurring theme in their history ever since. If Serbs and Albanians could forgive one another and act so as to be forgiven by one another they would have a future. If not, they were destined to replay the Battle of 1389 until the end of time.[1]

Nothing is more dispiriting than the cycle of revenge that haunts conflict zones and traps their populations into a past that never relaxes its grip. That has been the fate of the Balkans, Northern Ireland, India and Kashmir, the Middle East. The virus of hate can lie dormant for a while, but it rarely dies. Instead it mutates. Under a dictatorship, Serbs and Croats had lived together peaceably for 50 years. They had become friends and neighbours. But, as in virtually every other zone of historical conflict, something happens – there is a shift in the power structure; a totalitarian government that had held local populations together by fear disintegrates; an episode occurs in which the members of one side commit an atrocity against the other – and it is as if the years of coexistence had never been. Friends become enemies; neighbours, antagonists. A wall of separation is then the least bad outcome, and even that often fails to end the violence.

Retaliation is the instinctual response to perceived wrong. Montesquieu wrote that 'every religion which is persecuted becomes itself persecuting; for as soon as by some accidental turn it arises from persecution, it attacks the religion which persecuted it'.[2] Nationalism, said Isaiah Berlin, 'is usually the product of a wound inflicted by one nation on the pride or territory of another'.[3] Historic grievances are rarely forgotten. They become part of a people's collective memory, the narrative parents tell their children, the story from which a group draws its sense of identity. A note of injustice not yet avenged is written into the script which is then re-enacted at moments of crisis. That is what makes conflict the default option between ancient antagonists, however many years of relative peace have intervened. 'No man', said Ogden Nash, 'ever forgets – where he buried the hatchet.'

It is this that makes forgiveness so counterintuitive an idea. It is more than a technique of conflict resolution. It is a stunningly original strategy. In a world without forgiveness, evil begets evil, harm generates harm, and there is no way short of exhaustion or forgetfulness of breaking the sequence. Forgiveness breaks the chain. It introduces into the logic of interpersonal encounter the unpredictability of grace. It represents a decision not to do what instinct and passion urge us to do. It answers hate with a refusal to hate, animosity with generosity. Few more daring ideas have ever entered the human situation. Forgiveness means that we are not destined endlessly to replay the grievances of yesterday. It is the ability to live with the past without being held captive by the past. It would not be an exaggeration to say that forgiveness is the most compelling testimony to human freedom. It is about the action that is not reaction. It is the refusal to be defined by circumstance. It represents our ability to change course, reframe the narrative of the past and create an unexpected set of possibilities for the future. Hannah Arendt understood this:

> The possible redemption from the predicament of irreversibility – of being unable to undo what one has done though one did not, and could not, have known what he was doing – is the faculty of forgiving ... [F]orgiving serves to undo the deeds of the past, whose 'sins' hang like Damocles' sword over every new generation ...[4]

In the face of tragedy, forgiveness is the counternarrative of hope. It is not a moral luxury, an option for saints. At times it is the only path through the thickets of hate to the open spaces of coexistence. I can still remember my undergraduate days, when I would return after a vacation, laden with luggage. In those days I couldn't afford a taxi, so I used to carry my heavy cases from the station to my college. They were so heavy that still, when I recall those days, I can feel the aching muscles and numb wrists. That is what it is to carry hate, resentment and a sense of grievance. They weigh us down. They stop us thinking of anything else. We may feel righteous. Indeed there is none so self-righteous as one who carries the burden of self-perceived victimhood. But it is ultimately dehumanizing. More than hate destroys the hated, it destroys the hater.

Forgiveness is, in origin, a religious virtue. There is no such thing as forgiveness in nature. The elements are blind, and the laws of nature inexorable. Famine, drought, disease, starvation make no exceptions for the virtuous or the penitent. The supreme poets of an unforgiving world were the dramatists of ancient Greece. For them, fate rules the destinies of mankind. To attempt to subvert or circumnavigate it is hubris which ends in nemesis. A world of impersonal forces is a tragically configured universe.

The prophets and visionaries of the Hebrew Bible have often been credited with the discovery of monotheism, the idea that there is only one God. That, I suspect, is a less significant discovery than its other great insight: that God is *personal*, that there is something at the heart of reality that responds to and affirms our existence as persons. The universe is more than a billion galaxies silently rotating in space. We are not mere cosmic dust on the surface of eternity. We are here because someone wanted us to be. God did not create the universe as a scientist in a laboratory, or as a technocrat setting in motion the big bang but rather as a parent giving birth to a child. The universe is neither indifferent nor hostile to our existence. That was the great leap of the biblical imagination.

At the heart of the concept of forgiveness is the idea of love – not abstract love but the real, concrete attachment of one being for another. Love distinguishes between the person and the deed. An act may be evil, but since the person is free, he or she is not inseparably joined to that evil. Wrongdoing damages the structures of our world. It creates an injustice. It damages a relationship. But these things are not beyond repair. Wrongs can be rectified, and harm healed. And when the wrongdoer expresses remorse, apologizes and undertakes not to repeat the wrong, he or she testifies to the fact that they are no longer identified with what they have done. Forgiveness is, and can only be, a relationship between free persons: between the forgiven, who has shown that he or she can change, and the forgiver who has faith that the other person will change. Freedom – the ability to act in unpredictable ways – is the refutation of tragedy.

The paradigm of forgiveness is the love between parent and

child. A parent knows that a child will make mistakes. True parenthood is the willingness, at a certain stage, to empower a child to make mistakes, for without this no child can become mature and responsible. Forgiveness is that empowerment, because it means that the child is safe in the knowledge that no error is final, no wrongdoing the end of a relationship. Not accidentally the Hebrew word *rachamim*, meaning mercy or the capacity to forgive, comes from the word *rechem*, meaning a womb. A judge, charged with administering the law, cannot forgive, but a parent can. The concept of forgiveness comes into existence when God is envisaged as both judge and parent; when law and love, justice and mercy, join hands. God forgives, and in so doing, teaches us to forgive.

* * *

One of the most fascinating discoveries of sociobiology has been to provide scientific insight into the role of forgiveness. Already in an earlier chapter we described the application of games theory to the question of group survival in the face of uncertainty. By repeated applications of the Prisoner's Dilemma it became possible to chart the consequences of different ways of relating to others. As we noted, the first discovery was the effectiveness of the strategy known as Tit-for-Tat, or reciprocal altruism, the principle of 'measure for measure'. Mathematicians quickly discovered, however, that Tit-for-Tat has a fateful weakness. When it meets a spiteful opponent ('Always defect') it gets drawn into a spiral of retaliation.

In the late 1980s a Polish mathematician, Martin Nowak, devised a program that was more effective than Tit-for-Tat. It involved a small modification of the original program. Randomly, but on average once every three or so moves, it overlooked the last move of its opponent. It had to do so randomly because if its behaviour was predictable it could be taken into account by a ruthless predator. None the less the strategy was effective in remedying the great defect of its predecessor, namely the trap of retaliation, while retaining its immunity to exploitation by defectors. Nowak called his program Generous. What he had done was essentially to create a computer simulation of reconciliation. *Forgetting* is as close as a computer gets to *forgiving*.[5]

Recall that the original Tit-for-Tat was a model of retributive justice: as you do to others so shall it be done unto you. Nowak's new approach to the Iterated Prisoner's Dilemma was to add a further element to the equation: the ability to overlook or disregard at least some of the hostile moves made against you. What Nowak had done was, in effect, to rediscover the ancient truth articulated by Judaism's sages: 'In the beginning, God sought to create the world through the attribute of justice, but He saw that it could not stand. What then did He do? He took justice and joined to it the attribute of mercy.'[6]

* * *

Forgiveness is a complex idea, and its emergence in Jewish sensibility is a drama in five acts, each adding a new dimension to the concept's richness. The first appears early in the Bible. Human beings have become corrupt. The world is 'filled with violence' and God 'regrets that He had made man on earth'. He brings a flood, and only Noah and his family survive. Emerging from the ark, Noah brings an offering to God, who is moved to compassion. 'Never again will I curse the ground because of man, even though every inclination of his heart is evil from childhood.' This determination is made the basis of a covenant whose sign is the rainbow: 'Whenever I bring clouds over the earth and the rainbow appears in the clouds, I will remember My covenant between Me and you and all living creatures of every kind. Never again will the waters become a flood to destroy all life.' This is forgiveness as an act of grace, a unilateral decision on the part of God. There has been no apology, no remorse, no act of restitution. Those who might have done so, died in the flood. Noah, the survivor, was righteous and had no cause to be contrite. The rainbow covenant is a declaration, as it were, of pre-emptive forgiveness. God binds Himself in advance to temper justice with mercy. He accepts that He cannot expect perfection from mankind.

The second act – the Bible's most extended essay on the

concept of forgiveness – is about the relationship between human beings. Joseph, eleventh of Jacob's sons, is envied by his brothers. They resent his dreams and airs of grandeur. They are jealous of the fact that Jacob seems to love him more than them. The richly embroidered robe he gives Joseph acts as a constant provocation. Alone with Joseph while tending the sheep, they plot to kill him and eventually they sell him into slavery. After many vicissitudes, Joseph becomes second-in-command in Egypt and a long drama ensues, throughout the whole of which the brothers fail to recognize his true identity. Finally Joseph discloses who he is, and when they are silenced by the shock, he tells them, 'Do not be distressed or feel guilty because you sold me. Look! God has sent me ahead of you to save lives.' It is a momentous gesture of forgiveness, but it is not enough to allay the brothers' fear. Evidently they believe he is constrained by one of the rules of a blood feud, that brothers do not execute vengeance against one another during their father's lifetime. When Jacob dies, Joseph therefore repeats his forgiveness, this time with greater force: 'Don't be afraid. Am I in the place of God? You intended to harm me, but God intended it for good.'

The Joseph story is one of the definitive narratives of the Hebrew Bible. Long, detailed and highly structured, it brings to closure one of the motifs of the Book of Genesis, namely sibling rivalry. We tend to forget that *fraternity*, a key word of modern politics, is anything but a straightforward virtue. The archetypal relationships in Genesis – Cain and Abel, Isaac and Ishmael, Jacob and Esau, Joseph and his brothers – are fraught with conflict and animosity. 'How good and pleasant it is when brothers live together in unity' says the Book of Psalms, to which one is tempted to add, 'and how rare!' Yet there is an identifiable progression. Cain kills Abel. Isaac and Ishmael live apart. Jacob and Esau, after a tense and troubled time, part and eventually meet, many years later, in reconciliation. Esau has forgotten his grievance. With Joseph, forgiveness enters the scene and heralds a new way forward. Sibling rivalry is not fated to end in tragedy as long as one of the partners is able to say, 'You intended to harm me, but God intended it for good.'

The Joseph story does more than bring the concept of forgiveness from God to mankind. It also establishes the precondition of forgiveness. Between the brothers' first meeting in Egypt and Joseph's eventual disclosure of his identity, an intricate series of actions takes place. Joseph accuses the brothers of being spies and demands that they bring their youngest, Benjamin, with them next time. He plants money in their sacks and eventually his silver chalice, allowing him to accuse Benjamin of theft and threatening to imprison him. The meaning of this otherwise unfathomable set of digressions is simple. Joseph wants to see if the brothers are capable of repentance and remorse. They are. After the first accusation, they say – unaware that Joseph is listening – 'We deserve to be punished because of what we did to our brother.' At the second encounter, as Benjamin is about to be sentenced, Judah pleads, 'Let me remain as your slave in place of the lad.' The significance is that it was Judah who, years earlier, had proposed selling Joseph into slavery. Now he is willing to suffer that fate rather than see a brother be made a slave. Judah becomes the prototype of penitence, just as Joseph becomes the archetype of forgiveness.

The third act is high religious drama. The Israelites have become a people. Rescued from slavery in Egypt, they receive their constitution in the form of the revelation at Mount Sinai. It is not long, though, before they fall from the heights. In Moses' absence they make and worship a golden calf. Moses pleads to God to forgive them. As he descends from the mountain and sees the people cavorting before the idol, he smashes the tablets of stone, carved by God, on which the laws of the covenant have been inscribed. After a further 40 days and nights of intercession, God agrees to forgive the people and instructs Moses to carve a second set of tablets. These become the symbol of reconciliation, and in later Jewish tradition the basis of an annual day of repentance and forgiveness, namely the Day of Atonement, the anniversary of the day on which Moses brought the second tablets to the people. Moses' prayer introduces the idea of *collective* atonement. Not only individuals, but a people, can be forgiven.

The fourth stage takes forgiveness into the arena of international relations. In one of his speeches to the next generation, Moses instructs the Israelites: 'Do not despise an Egyptian, for you were strangers in his land.'[7] This is an astonishing remark. Egypt, in the Mosaic books, is the epitome of oppression. It was where the Israelites were enslaved, and where they suffered the first attempted genocide against them. Moses' command is surpassing in its wisdom. To be free, he suggests, is not merely to be liberated from a tyrant; it is to refuse to be held captive by memory. If the Israelites were to harbour a grievance against their former enemies, they would still be slaves, if not in body then at least in mind. He instructs them to let go of hate and desire for revenge.

In the fifth stage, forgiveness is integrated into the texture of religious life. It is no longer optional, contingent on the promptings of the heart. It becomes part of the cycle of the year. The Day of Atonement is time dedicated to reconciliation between ourselves and God, and between us and other people. One of the principles of forgiveness is that it can only be granted by the party against whom wrong was committed. Jewish law drew the radical conclusion, that God Himself can only forgive offences against Himself. 'For transgressions between man and God, the Day of Atonement atones. But for transgressions between man and his fellow man, the Day of Atonement does not atone until he has obtained forgiveness from his fellow man.'[8] Thus, the days leading up to the Day of Atonement became an annual period of apology, restitution and forgiveness.

In general, Jewish law set a high value on reconciliation and knew the dangers if it was not forthcoming. One of the examples given by Maimonides is the biblical story of Absolom and Amnon. Amnon had raped Absolom's sister Tamar. At the time, Absolom said nothing. He appeared to have either forgiven or forgotten the offence. Two years later, however, Absolom took his revenge and had Amnon killed. Silence is no evidence of forgiveness. Better, concludes Maimonides, to confront the wrongdoer directly:

> When someone sins against another, the offended party should not hate him and remain silent. This is what is said about the wicked: 'And Absolom spoke to Amnon neither

good nor evil, although Absolom hated Amnon.' Rather, he is commanded to speak to him and say to him, 'Why did you do this to me? Why did you sin against me in such-and-such a matter?' Thus it is said, 'You shall surely rebuke your neighbour.' If he repents and requests forgiveness, then one must forgive and not be harsh.[9]

This is not always necessary. To forgive without the dialectic of accusation and apology, as an unconditional act of grace, is equally mandated, and a sign of moral greatness:

If someone is sinned against by another and the offended party does not wish to rebuke him or to say anything to him – perhaps because the sinner is simple-minded or distraught – then if one forgives him in his heart and bears no animosity against him and does not rebuke him, this is indeed the way of saintliness [*middat hassidut*].[10]

For Maimonides, as for other interpreters of Jewish law, the biblical prohibition, 'Do not seek revenge or bear a grudge' was an essential precondition of social existence:

If one bears a grudge about something and remembers it, then one may come to take revenge. Therefore the Torah was particularly concerned [to avoid] grudge-bearing so that the wrong done should be completely blotted out from a person's heart and not remembered. This is the appropriate character trait and makes possible the settlement of the earth and social relations among human beings.[11]

* * *

Judaism is often portrayed as a religion of justice rather than mercy and forgiveness. That, I hope I have shown, is not the case. Justice and forgiveness go hand-in-hand. Each is an answer to the problem of revenge, and neither is sufficient on its own. Justice takes the sense of wrong and transforms it from personal retaliation – revenge – to the impersonal processes of law –

retribution. Forgiveness is the further acknowledgement that justice alone may not be enough to silence the feelings of the afflicted. Even when the evidence has been taken, the verdict passed, and sentence imposed, there is a residue of pain and grief which has to be discharged. Justice is the impersonal, forgiveness the personal, restoration of moral order. Justice rights wrongs; forgiveness rebuilds broken relationships. There is, as Maimonides says, no other way.

It is impossible to understand the force of forgiveness without, at the same time, acknowledging its difficulty. It is hard precisely because it conflicts with our sense of keeping faith with the past. If wrong has been done to me, it is natural to feel that wrong must be done to the wrongdoer in return. When that wrong is historic – when its victims are no longer alive – we feel that more than mere justice is at stake. Only the offended party can forgive, and he or she is no longer alive to be able to forgive. We, the family or friends of the victim, feel the pull of loyalty to the unappeased cry of those who are no longer here. Forgiveness can then come to seem like a betrayal. Michael Ignatieff has understood this well:

> The chief moral obstacle in the path of reconciliation is the desire for revenge. Now, revenge is commonly regarded as a low and unworthy emotion, and because it is regarded as such, its deep moral hold on people is rarely understood. But revenge – morally considered – is a desire to keep faith with the dead, to honour their memory by taking up their cause where they left off. Revenge keeps faith between generations; the violence it engenders is a ritual form of respect for the community's dead – therein lies its legitimacy. Reconciliation is difficult precisely because it must compete with the powerful alternative morality of violence. Political terror is tenacious because it is an ethical practice. It is a cult of the dead, a dire and absolute expression of respect.[12]

How then is forgiveness possible? It is possible because, once the impartial processes of law have taken their course, justice done, sentences served, amends made and apologies expressed, a halt must be called to the otherwise endless voice of implacable grief. Forgiveness does not mean forgetting, nor does it mean abandoning the claims of justice. It does mean, however, an acknowledgement that the past is past and must not be allowed to cast its shadow over the future. Forgiveness heals moral wounds the way the body heals physical wounds. At its height it is a process of shared mourning between those who commit and those who suffer the consequences of wrong; the former for harm done, the latter for harm suffered – and like all acts of mourning it is the only bridge from the pain of loss to reintegration with the present and its tasks.

* * *

Laura Blumenfeld is a young American Jew. In 1986 her father, a rabbi, was visiting Jerusalem. While walking in the Old City, he was shot by a Palestinian terrorist. The bullet missed his brain by half an inch. Seriously injured, he survived. His daughter, however, could not forget or forgive. Years later, by then a journalist, she travelled to Israel, and without disclosing her identity, befriended the family of the gunman and began a correspondence with the terrorist himself, now in jail. Not knowing that he was speaking to the victim's daughter, the father of the gunman explained why his son shot an American stranger: 'He did his duty. Every Palestinian must do it. Then there will be justice.' Another son added: 'My brother never met the man personally. It's not a personal issue. Nothing personal, so no revenge.' Laura writes in her diary, 'The heat was rising in my face. It was personal. It was personal to me.'

She attends the terrorist's trial and persuades counsel – still without revealing who she is – to let her give testimony. On the witness stand she finally discloses the fact that she is the victim's daughter and that she has come to know the gunman and his family so that they can put a personal face to the family of the injured man and understand that there is no such thing as an impersonal victim of violence. In the middle of her cross-examination, she is interrupted by another voice:

A woman stood up at the back of the courtroom. She blurted out in English, in a loud, shaking voice, 'I forgive Omar for what he did.'

Forgive? It was my mother. This was not about forgiveness; didn't she understand? This was my revenge.

'And if the Blumenfeld family can forgive Omar,' my mother continued, 'it's time for the State of Israel to forgive him.'[13]

The two women leave the court in tears, but the family of the gunman run after them and embrace. Later the gunman writes to Laura, 'We have been in a state of war and now we are passing through a new stage of historical reconciliation where there is no place for hatred and detestation.'

Was anything achieved in this confrontation? The issues at stake in the Middle East are intractable and have defied every attempt at a solution. Yet there can be little doubt that a solution exists: a division of the land into two states, roughly coinciding with existing centres of population, an agreement about Jerusalem and holy sites so that each has access to places important to them, joint supervision of shared resources such as water, and an international accord about the future of displaced refugees. The question is: is there a solution that would be acceptable to both sides? Both have long memories, Israelis of 2,000 years of Jewish suffering and the existential need for Jews to have, somewhere on earth, defensible space; Palestinians of displacement and loss, political impotence and economic hardship, of humiliating defeat and anger. These are two narratives, neither of which makes space for the other. As in so many other conflict zones, deadlock recapitulates the classic terms of the Prisoner's Dilemma. An absence of trust leads both parties to courses of action which, rational in themselves, end in consequences disastrous to both. Forgiveness seems absurdly inadequate to substantive conflicts of interest and the sheer momentum of suspicion, distrust and cumulative grievance.

Yet in the end peace is made, if at all, then by people who acknowledge the personhood of their opponents. Until Israelis and Palestinians are able to listen to one another, hear each other's anguish and anger and make cognitive space for one another's hopes, there is no way forward. One of the great stories of the Bible is about how King Solomon decided who was the real mother when two women came before him, each claiming that the baby in front of them was her child. The true mother, he understood, was the one who was prepared to give the child away rather than let it be killed. Love is more than possession; it is in part the ability to let go. Forgiveness is the ability to let go, and without it we kill what we most love. Every act of forgiveness mends something broken in this fractured world. It is a step, however small, in the long, hard journey to redemption.

I am a Jew. As a Jew I carry with me the tears and sufferings of my grandparents and theirs through the generations. The story of my people is a narrative of centuries of exiles and expulsions, persecutions and pogroms, beginning with the First Crusade and culminating in the murder of two-thirds of Europe's Jews, among them more than a million children. For centuries, Jews knew that they or their children risked being murdered simply because they were Jews. Those tears are written into the very fabric of Jewish memory, which is to say, Jewish identity. How can I let go of that pain when it is written into my very soul?

And yet I must. For the sake of my children and theirs, not yet born. Hating the German people will not bring back to life one victim of the Holocaust. Hating the Palestinians will not bring Israel one step nearer to peace. Loving God more does not entitle me to love people less. Asking God to forgive me, I hear, in the very process of making that request, His demand of me that I forgive others. I forgive because I have a duty to the future no less than to the past – to my children as well as to my ancestors. Indeed the former defines the latter. The duty I owe my ancestors who died because of their faith is to build a world in which people no longer die because of their faith. I honour the past not by repeating it but by learning from it – by refusing to add pain to pain, grief to grief. That is why we must answer hatred with love, violence with peace, resentment with generosity of spirit and conflict with reconciliation.

NOTES

1. On forgiveness and conciliation, see Johnston and Sampson 1994; Shriver 1995; Baum and Wells 1997; Etzioni and Carney 1997; Enright and North 1998; Gopin 2000; and Henderson 2002.
2. Montesquieu, *The Spirit of Laws*, Book XXV, Chapter 9.
3. Berlin 2002, p. 347.
4. Quoted in Shriver, 1995, p. 34.
5. Ridley 1996, pp. 76–8.
6. Rashi to Genesis 1: 1.
7. Deuteronomy 23: 8.
8. Mishnah, *Yoma*, 9.
9. Maimonides, Mishnah Torah, Laws of Ethical Character (*Hilkhot Deot*), 6: 6.
10. Ibid., 6: 9.
11. Ibid., 7: 8.
12. Ignatieff 1997, p. 188.
13. *The Times*, 25, 26 March 2002.

Chapter 11

A Covenant of Hope

Suppose that the world's author put the case to you before creation, saying: 'I am going to make a world not certain to be saved, a world the perfection of which shall be conditional merely, the condition being that each several agent does its own "level best". I offer you the chance to take part in such a world. Its safety, you see, is unwarranted. It is a real adventure, with real danger, yet it may win through. It is a social scheme of co-operative work genuinely to be done. Will you join the procession? Will you trust yourself and trust the other agents sufficiently to face the risk?' [Or would you say] that, rather than be part and parcel of so fundamentally pluralist and irrational a universe, you preferred to relapse into the slumber of nonentity from which you had been momentarily aroused by the tempter's voice?

(William James, *Pragmatism*)

There is nothing inevitable about the survival of civilizations. The pages of history are littered with the debris of empires that seemed impregnable in their day but soon thereafter fell into decay and oblivion. It has been my thesis that the opportunities posed by global capitalism and the power of technology are vast and potentially benign. They herald the alleviation of poverty, the defeat of ignorance and the treatment of disease on an unprecedented scale. The risks, however, are immense.

There is a real and present danger that the market, left to its own devices, will continue to concentrate wealth in fewer and fewer hands, leaving whole nations destitute and significant numbers of people, even within advanced economies, without stable employment, income or prospects. Envy, anger and the sheer sense of injustice are fertile soil for the growth of protest, violence and terror from which, given the openness on which globalization depends, none of us is immune. The steady erosion of families and communities leaves individuals without networks of support. The substitution of market price for moral value renders us inarticulate in the face of the random cruelties of fate.

Our habits of consumption are denuding the world of its natural resources, leaving future generations with ever less on which to survive. Our despoliation of the environment threatens more species with extinction than at any time since *homo sapiens* first set foot on earth. Global warming endangers the biosphere. Genetic intervention in the food chain poses unquantifiable risks to health. Eugenic cloning and other medical technologies may lead humanity to promethean alterations of the human genome, privileging the few at the cost of the many and calling into question the very idea of human uniqueness and irreplaceability on which our ideas of love, the human person and the non-negotiable dignity of a human life depend. Beyond these and no less urgent is the growing fragmentation of politics, the rise of new forms of tribalism and religious extremism, the persistence of ethnic wars and the capacity of highly decentralized groups, sometimes no more than a few individuals, to put security of life at risk. We have a global economy. We do not yet have a global culture, global governance or a coherent vision of global concern.

* * *

The wisdom of the world's religions may seem at best irrelevant, at worst dangerous, to a world driven by economic forces. In the West, especially Western Europe, society has become secularized. In the Middle East and parts of Asia it has witnessed a growth of fundamentalism that threatens economic development and political freedom alike. Whatever therefore the prospects for the future, religion seems too powerless to effect change or too powerful to be constrained by it. Either way, it seems destined to be part of the problem rather than part of the solution.

This view, I believe, is a mistake, though it is one with a distinguished pedigree. Two of the most influential works of Western modernity – Hobbes' *Leviathan* and Adam Smith's *The Wealth of Nations* – were predicated on the idea of man the maximizing animal. Politically this led to the social contract; economically to the division of labour and the free market. Mankind, however, is not merely a maximizing animal. We are also, uniquely, the meaning-seeking animal. We seek to understand our place in the universe. We want to know where we have come from, where we are going to, and of what narrative we are a part. We form families, communities and societies. We tell stories, some of which have the status of sacred texts. We perform rituals that dramatize the structure of reality. We have languages, cultures, moralities and faiths. These things are essential to our sense of continuity with the past and responsibility to the future. Without them it is doubtful whether we would have reasons for action at all beyond the most minimal drives for survival. That is why religion is a persisting feature of the human situation, and will not disappear so long as we ask the most fundamental questions of why we are here and what kind of world we seek to create.

Part of the process we call modernity – most obviously associated with the European Enlightenment – was to call into question the salience of almost everything associated with the word 'religion'. *Écrasez l'infâme*, said Voltaire, and others, less provocatively, agreed. The new paradigm was science which rested its conclusions not on weightless clouds of revelation and prophetic insight but on testable hypotheses, experiments and refutations. Technology would help us master nature. Constitutional monarchy, followed by representative democracy, would control power. Economics would maximize wealth. Together they would generate the linear advance that went by the new name of 'progress'.

That was a noble aspiration and much of it remains valid today. But mankind is now older, sadder and wiser. Reason did not dispel prejudice. Technology, whether in the form of weapons of mass destruction, over-exploitation of natural resources, pollution of the atmosphere, or genetic manipulation, threatens the sustainability of nature itself. Representative democracy remains the best form of government yet discovered, but nation-states seem increasingly unable to control global phenomena from multinational corporations to ecological devastation, and we have not yet evolved a form of global governance. Market capitalism has increased wealth beyond the imagination of previous generations, but cannot, in and of itself, distribute it equally or even equitably. These are problems that cannot be solved within the terms set by modernity, for the simple reason that they are not procedural, but rather valuational or, to use the simple word, moral. There is no way of bypassing difficult moral choices by way of a scientific decision–procedure that states: 'Maximize X.' We first have to decide which X we wish to maximize, and how to weigh X against Y when the pursuit of one damages the fulfilment of the other. The human project is inescapably a moral project. That is one reason why the great faiths, with their history of reflection on moral issues, must be part of the conversation.

Economic superpowers, seemingly invincible in their time, have a relatively short life-span: Venice in the sixteenth century, the Netherlands in the seventeenth, France in the eighteenth, Britain in the nineteenth and the United States in the twentieth. The great religions, by contrast, survive. Islam is 1,500 years old, Christianity 2,000 and Judaism 4,000. Why this should be so is open to debate. My own view is that the world faiths embody truths unavailable to economics and politics, and they remain salient even when everything else changes. They remind us that civilizations survive not by strength but by how they respond to the weak; not by wealth but by the care they show for the poor; not by power but by their concern for the powerless. The ironic yet utterly humane lesson of history is that what renders a culture invulnerable is the compassion it shows to the vulnerable. The ultimate value we should be concerned to maximize is human dignity – the dignity of all human beings, equally, as children of the creative, redeeming God.

Is this a 'religious' insight? Yes and no. There have been

secular humanists who have affirmed it; there have been religious zealots who have denied it. What matters most is not why we hold it, but that we hold it. Global capitalism heralds the prospect of a vast amelioration of the human condition. Equally it threatens inequalities that will eventually become unsustainable and cultural vandalism that will become unbearable. Man was not made for the service of economies; economies were made to serve mankind; and men and women were made – so I believe – to serve one another, not just themselves. We may not survive while others drown; we may not feast while others starve; we are not free when others are in servitude; we are not well when billions languish in disease and premature death.

* * *

But religion enters the conversation for another reason as well, and credit is due to Francis Fukuyama for drawing attention to it. In his famous 1989 essay, 'The End of History', written in the wake of the collapse of the Cold War, he argued that the world was moving inexorably toward free markets and free societies, to what Michael Novak calls 'democratic capitalism'.[1] That view has been shaken – not necessarily refuted but certainly compromised – by events since: proliferating ethnic and religious conflicts, the failure of the Oslo Peace Process in the Middle East, above all by September 11.

However, Fukuyama later wrote a book under the same title, and gave a more nuanced presentation of his case. In the final chapter he raised the possibility that history may have no end, precisely because every peaceful order generates, by the sheer capriciousness of human character, its own disruption. 'The decline of community life suggests that in the future we risk becoming secure and self-absorbed last men', he wrote. 'But the opposite danger exists as well, namely that we will return to being first men engaged in bloody and pointless prestige battles, only this time with modern weapons.'[2]

The very thing that first commended capitalism to its advocates – the fact that it took people's minds away from war and led them instead to the pursuit of trade – constitutes, to its critics, its shortcomings. The virtues of a liberal democratic order are, from another perspective, its vices. People turn away from public life to private devices and desires. They become self-absorbed, domesticated, bourgeois. They no longer ally themselves to the great causes that once called forth patriotism, loyalty, the willingness to sacrifice oneself for the sake of one's country or one's faith. But the urge to these passions does not die. It remains as a genetic residue from an earlier age when men had to fight battles to survive. The danger, therefore, is that a primordial instinct will resurface in revolt against market capitalism's taming of the human instinct to violence:

> Supposing that the world has become 'filled up' so to speak, with liberal democracies, such that there exist no tyranny and oppression worthy of the name against which to struggle? Experience suggests that if men cannot struggle on behalf of a just cause because that just cause was victorious in an earlier generation, then they will struggle *against* that just cause. They will struggle for the sake of struggle. They will struggle, in other words, out of a certain boredom: for they cannot imagine living in a world without struggle. And if the greater part of the world in which they live is characterized by peaceful and prosperous liberal democracy, then they will struggle *against* that peace and prosperity, and against democracy.[3]

That danger has become real in ways that were not obvious in 1992 when Fukuyama wrote those words. Then it seemed as if the primary actors on the global stage were nation-states. Since then it has become possible, through the combination of the Internet, satellite phones and encrypted e-mails – techniques used in the September 11 attacks – to mobilize globally at a level far below that of nation-states, and yet still create panic and disruption, undermining the securities and confidences on which everyday life depends.

It is far easier to monitor and defend oneself against states than to do so for 'super-empowered individuals'. Such individuals –

Osama bin Laden is the paradigm, but there are many others – fit Fukuyama's description. They come from well-to-do, even affluent families. They are themselves products of the system they set out to destroy. The real danger comes when they attempt to mobilize, not a cadre of like-minded individuals, but large and globally dispersed groups. It is then that the power of religion becomes real and frightening. For the world faiths, especially Christianity and Islam, *are* global phenomena. Between them they command the loyalties of more than half the earth's six billion inhabitants, many of whom have quite different grievances against global capitalism. Often they are poor and unemployed. They live under repressive regimes. Constant images of the wealthy and (by traditional standards) decadent West, conveyed by television and the Internet, inflame both envy and hostility. If the personal animus of elite individuals can be turned into a populist religious struggle against the infidel, the unbeliever, the 'great Satan', then we have the beginnings of a scenario perilously close to Huntington's prediction of a clash of civilizations. It is not too much to say that this is the greatest danger threatening the twenty-first century.

We are radically unprepared for this challenge, and this too Fukuyama understood. Absent religious faith, add the failure of the 'Enlightenment project' to create a universal ethic, and the result is moral relativism – a way of thinking (or rather, refusing to think) about life choices that may be suited to a consumer culture, but one that is wholly inadequate to the defence of freedom in the face of passionate, violent and fanatical challenge:

> Modern thought raises no barriers to a future nihilistic war against liberal democracy on the part of those brought up in its bosom. Relativism – the doctrine that all values are merely relative and which attacks all 'privileged perspectives' – must ultimately end up undermining democratic and tolerant values as well. Relativism is not a weapon that can be aimed selectively at the enemies one chooses. It fires indiscriminately, shooting out the legs of not only the 'absolutisms', dogmas, and certainties of the Western tradition, but that tradition's emphasis on tolerance,

diversity, and freedom of thought as well. If nothing can
true absolutely, if all values are culturally determined, then
cherished principles like human equality have to go by the
wayside as well.[4]

Relativism is inadequate to the challenge of assertive ethnicities
and exclusive belief systems. Indeed, the very failure of relativism
to ground identity in something larger than the self gives rise to its
opposite – the search for belonging; and there is a link between
violence and belonging. 'The more strongly you feel the bonds of
belonging to your own group', writes Michael Ignatieff, 'the more
hostile, the more violent will your feelings be towards outsiders.
You can't have this intensity of belonging without violence,
because belonging of this intensity moulds the individual
conscience: if a nation gives people a reason to sacrifice
themselves, it also gives them a reason to kill.'[5] Those words,
written almost a decade before September 11 and the subsequent
spate of suicide bombings in the Middle East, reverberate with
ever greater urgency now.

In the aftermath of the European wars of religion in the
sixteenth and seventeenth centuries a doctrine was born which
laid the foundations for the modern nation-state. It was called
toleration. Essentially, it privatized conscience. It allowed that
people might belong to a civil and political order without
necessarily subscribing to the beliefs of the majority. Usually this
is thought of as part of a process of secularization. John
Plamenatz, however, rightly notes that in Milton, Locke and
others it had an essentially religious underpinning. It involved
moving from the view that 'Faith is supremely important, and
therefore all men must have the one true faith', to the proposition
that 'Faith is supremely important, and therefore every man must
be allowed to live by the faith which seems true to him.' This is
not relativism but a deeply religious understanding that faith
coerced is not faith; that religious worship must be free if it is to be
a genuine assent of the soul. 'Liberty of conscience', Plamenatz
writes, 'was born, not of indifference, not of scepticism, not of
mere open-mindedness, but of faith.'[6] That is what differentiates

century approach to liberty from twentieth-
s such as Friedrich Hayek, Karl Popper and
se latter-day thinkers predicated their ideas of a
cepticism and uncertainty, and in so doing
ence of liberty, making it vulnerable to those
...o ngilt in the name of certainty.

A return to the seventeenth-century concept of toleration is not enough. It was sufficient then because it went hand in hand with the strong central power of the state. Different groups were forced to live together because none was in a position to impose its view on others. Power had been centralized and delegated to an authority strong enough to ensure the rule of law. Globalization involves the opposite – decentralization of power combined with maximum vulnerability such that individual acts of terror can destabilize large parts of the world while remaining beyond the reach of any one state, even a superpower as dominant as the United States. Something far stronger than toleration is required.

I have argued that if we are to find an idea equal to the challenge of our time it must come from within the great religious traditions themselves. I have tried to articulate one possible form of that idea. It is that the one God, creator of diversity, commands us to honour his creation by respecting diversity. God, the parent of mankind, loves us as a parent loves – each child for what he or she uniquely is. The idea that one God entails one faith, one truth, one covenant, is countered by the story of Babel. That story is preceded by the covenant with Noah and thus with all mankind – the moral basis of a shared humanity, and thus ultimately of universal human rights. But it is followed by an assertion of the dignity of difference – of Abraham and his children who follow their diverging paths to his presence, each valued, each 'chosen', each loved, each blessed by God. Until the great faiths not merely tolerate but find positive value in the diversity of the human condition, we will have wars, and their cost in human lives will continue to rise.

There is nothing relativist about the idea of the dignity of difference. It is based on the radical transcendence of God from the created universe, with its astonishing diversity of life forms – all of which, as we now know through genetic research, derive from a single source – and from the multiple languages and cultures through which we, as meaning-seeking beings, have attempted to understand the totality of existence. Just as the human situation would be impoverished and unsustainable if we were to eliminate all life forms except our own, so it would be reduced and fatally compromised if we were to eliminate all cultural, civilizational and religious forms except our own. The idea that we fulfil God's will by waging war against the infidel, or converting the heathen, so that all humanity shares the same faith is an idea that – as I have tried to argue – owes much to the concept of empire and little to the heritage of Abraham, which Jews, Christians and Muslims claim as their own. It was not until the Abrahamic faith came into contact with Greek and Roman imperialism that it developed into an aspiration to conquer or convert the world, and we must abandon it if we are to save ourselves from mutual destruction. To repeat my formulation in an earlier chapter: fundamentalism, like imperialism, is the attempt to impose a single truth on a plural world. It is the Tower of Babel of our time.

The test of faith is whether I can make space for difference. Can I recognize God's image in someone who is not in my image, whose language, faith, ideals, are different from mine? If I cannot, then I have made God in my image instead of allowing him to remake me in his. Can Israeli make space for Palestinian, and Palestinian for Israeli? Can Muslims, Hindus, Sikhs, Confucians, Orthodox, Catholics and Protestants make space for one another in India, Sri Lanka, Chechnya, Kosovo and the dozens of other places in which different ethnic and religious groups exist in close proximity? Can we create a paradigm shift through which we come to recognize that we are enlarged, not diminished, by difference, just as we are enlarged, not diminished, by the 6,000 languages that exist today, each with its unique sensibilities, art forms and literary expressions? This is not the cosmopolitanism of those who belong nowhere, but the deep human understanding that passes between people who, knowing how important their attachments are to them, understand how deeply someone else's different attachments matter to them also.

* * *

With this I return to a concept that has underlain much of what I have argued – the concept of *covenant*. Initially a form of treaty between neighbouring powers in the ancient Near East, it became, in the Hebrew Bible, a – even the – central form of relationship, laden with religious and moral significance. Covenant is an answer to the most fundamental question in the evolution of societies: How can we establish relationships secure enough to become the basis of co-operation, without the use of economic, political or military power? The use of power is ruled out by the requirement of human dignity. If you and I are linked because, one way or another, I can force you to do what I want, then I have secured my freedom at the cost of yours. I have asserted my humanity by denying yours. Covenant is the attempt to create partnership without dominance or submission. It exists because of one extraordinary feature of language. We can use words to place ourselves under obligations. The great Oxford philosopher J. L. Austin called this 'performative utterance'. Covenant occurs when two individuals or groups, differing perhaps in power, but each acknowledging the integrity and sovereignty of the other, pledge themselves in mutual loyalty to achieve together what neither can achieve alone. Covenant is the use of language to create a bond of trust through the word given, the word received, the word honoured in mutual fidelity.

A covenant is not a contract. It differs in three respects. It is not limited to specific conditions and circumstances. It is open-ended and long-lasting. And it is not based on the idea of two individuals, otherwise unconnected, pursuing personal advantage. It is about the 'We' that gives identity to the 'I'. There is a place for contracts, but covenants are prior and more fundamental. They form the matrix of mutuality within which contractual relationships can exist. As Philip Selznick notes:

Every genuine covenant restates and reaffirms the basic

features of morality: deference to a source of judgement beyond autonomous will; constructive self-regard; concern for the well-being of others. At the same time, it establishes the principles of a *particular* way of life ... It is not an abstract morality.[7]

What makes covenant a concept for our time is that it affirms the dignity of difference. The great covenantal relationships – between God and mankind, between man and woman in marriage, between members of a community or citizens of a society – exist because both parties recognize that 'it is not good for man to be alone'. God cannot redeem the world without human participation; humanity cannot redeem the world without recognition of the divine. Man alone, and woman alone, cannot bring new life into the world. Members and citizens alone cannot sustain themselves, let alone establish a framework of collaborative action and collective grace. Covenants exist because we are different and seek to preserve that difference, even as we come together to bring our several gifts to the common good. They are brought into being because of the non-zero-sumness of relationship and interaction.

Covenants – because they are relational, not ontological – are inherently pluralistic. I have one kind of relationship with my parents, another with my spouse, others with my children, yet others with friends, neighbours, members of my faith, fellow citizens of my country, and with human beings wherever they suffer and need my help. None of these is exclusive. It is of the nature of real life, as opposed to philosophical abstraction, that we have many commitments and that they may, at times, conflict. But that is not inherently tragic, though it may give rise to regret, even grief. Pluralism is a form of hope, because it is founded in the understanding that precisely because we are different, each of us has something unique to contribute to the shared project of which we are a part. In the short term, our desires and needs may clash; but the very realization that difference is a source of blessing leads us to seek mediation, conflict resolution, conciliation and peace – the peace that is predicated on diversity, not on uniformity.

Covenant tells me that my faith is a form of relationship with

God – and that *one relationship does not exclude any other*, any more than parenthood excludes a love for all one's children. Nowhere is this more magnificently set out than in the vision of Isaiah in which the prophet sees a time in which the two great historical enemies of Israel's past – Egypt and Assyria – will one day become God's chosen alongside Israel itself:

> In that day there will be an altar to the Lord in the heart of Egypt, and a monument to the Lord at its border. It will be a sign and witness to the Lord Almighty in the land of Egypt. When they cry out to the Lord because of their oppressors, He will send them a saviour and defender, and He will rescue them ...
>
> In that day there will be a highway from Egypt to Assyria. The Assyrians will go to Egypt and the Egyptians to Assyria. The Egyptians and Assyrians will worship together. In that day Israel will be the third, along with Egypt and Assyria, a blessing on earth. The Lord Almighty will bless them, saying, 'Blessed be Egypt my people, Assyria my handiwork, and Israel my inheritance.' (Isaiah 19: 19–25)

This is an astonishing passage. Michael Fishbane calls it 'the most extreme transposition of a national historical memory conceivable'. Israel's unique deliverance, the exodus, is now to be repeated for its erstwhile enemies. Fishbane rightly notes that 'Isaiah has bequeathed to Egypt Israel's most personal memory for the sake of peace. The metamorphosis is stunning.'[8] Some 2,700 years before Horace Kallen coined the term 'pluralism', Isaiah had given it religious meaning. God's world is diverse. The paths to his presence are many. There are multiple universes of faith, each capturing something of the radiance of being and refracting it into the lives of its followers, none refuting or excluding the others, each as it were the native language of its followers, but combining in a hymn of glory to the creator.

Finally, covenants are intergenerational. 'Not with you alone who are standing here today in the presence of the Lord our God, am I making this covenant with its oath, but also with those who are not here today', says Moses at the end of his life (Deuteronomy 29: 14–15). A covenant is, in Edmund Burke's phrase, a partnership 'between those who are living, those who are dead, and those who are to be born'.[9] It reminds us that we are guardians of the past for the sake of the future. It extends our horizons to the chain of the generations of which we are a part. It holds us to the consequences of our actions, from exploitation of the environment to the over-commercialization of society to the utterly unforgivable arms trade and all the other ways in which self-interested conduct in the short term creates hazard in the long term. Covenant means extended responsibility, horizontally across space, vertically across time, to and for the totality of which we are a part.

* * *

Our global situation today is not unlike the condition of European nations during the great wars of religion of the sixteenth and seventeenth centuries in the wake of the Reformation. Then, as now, there were many societies riven by conflict. The question arose: how can people of violently conflicting beliefs live peaceably together? Out of that crisis came the idea – variously framed by Hobbes, Locke and Rousseau – of a social contract by which individuals agree to cede certain private powers to a central authority charged with the maintenance of order and pursuit of the common good.

We are not in sight of a global contract whereby nation-states agree to sacrifice part of their sovereignty to create a form of world governance. There is, however, an alternative, namely a global *covenant*. Covenants are more foundational than contracts. Social covenants create societies; social contracts create states. Ancient Israel initiated its social contract when, at the request of the people, Samuel anointed Saul as king, giving rise to Israel's first national government. It received its social covenant several centuries earlier in the revelation at Mount Sinai. The relation between covenant and contract is akin to that between the American Declaration of Independence (1776) and the Constitution (1789). The latter specifies the constitutional structure of the state, the former the moral principles of the society on which it is founded. Covenants are beginnings, acts of moral engagement. They are couched in broad terms whose precise meaning is the subject of ongoing debate but which stand as touchstones, ideals, reference points against which policies and practices are judged. What we need now is not a contract bringing into being a global political structure, but rather a covenant framing our shared vision for the future of humanity.

One idea links the first chapter of Genesis to the Declaration of Independence, namely that 'all men are created equal'. Philip Selznick's articulation of this idea seems to me compelling: 'Moral equality', he writes, 'is the postulate that all persons have the same intrinsic worth. They are unequal in talents, in contributions to social life, and in valid claims to rewards and resources. But everyone who is a person is presumptively entitled to recognition of that personhood.' Accordingly, each is entitled to 'the basic conditions that make life possible, tolerable and hopeful' – to what they need to sustain 'their dignity and integrity as persons'.[10] That is at least a starting point for a global covenant in which the nations of the world collectively express their commitment not only to human rights but also to human responsibilities, and not merely a political, but also an economic, environmental, moral and cultural conception of the common good, constructed on the twin foundations of shared humanity and respect for diversity.

One of the most important distinctions I have learned in the course of reflection on Jewish history is the difference between *optimism* and *hope*. Optimism is the belief that things will get better. Hope is the faith that, together, we can make things better. Optimism is a passive virtue, hope an active one. It takes no courage to be an optimist, but it takes a great deal of courage to have hope. Knowing what we do of our past, no Jew can be an optimist. But Jews have never – despite a history of sometimes awesome suffering – given up hope. Not by accident did they call the national anthem of their new state 'Hatikvah', meaning, the hope.

Hope does not exist in a conceptual vacuum, nor is it available to all configurations of culture. It is born in the belief that the sources of action lie within ourselves. We are not unwitting products of blind causes: the selfish gene, the Darwinian struggle for survival, the Hegelian dialectic of history, the Marxist war of classes, the Nietzschean clash of wills, a Durkheim set of sociological trends, or a Freudian complex of psychological drives of which we are only dimly aware. Humanity has never been at a loss for worldviews that place the source of action outside ourselves, casting our fate to the winds and tides of fortune which at best we can hope to appease, at worst we can resign ourselves to. Hope is the knowledge that we can choose; that we can learn from our mistakes and act differently next time; that history is not what Joseph Heller called it, a 'trashbag of random coincidences blown open by the wind', but a long, slow journey to redemption, whatever the digressions and false turns along the way.

Hope is a human virtue, but one with religious underpinnings. At its ultimate it is the belief not that God has written the script of history, that He will intervene to save us from the error of our ways or protect us from the worst consequences of evil, but simply that He is mindful of our aspirations, with us in our fumbling efforts, that He has given us the means to save us from ourselves; that we are not wrong to dream, wish and work for a better world. In the end, great systems of thought are self-validating. To one who believes that the human condition is essentially tragic, the human condition will reveal itself as a series of tragedies. To one who believes that we can rewrite the script, history reveals itself as a series of slow, faltering steps to a more gracious social order.

I believe that we can no longer, as religious leaders, assume that nothing has changed in the human situation. Something *has* changed: our power for good and evil, the sheer reach and consequences of our interventions. We have come face to face with the stranger, and it makes all the difference whether we find this threatening or enlarging. Every great faith has within it harsh texts which, read literally, can be taken to endorse narrow particularism, suspicion of strangers, and intolerance toward those who believe differently than we do. Every great faith also has within it sources that emphasize kinship with the stranger, empathy with the outsider, the courage that leads people to extend a hand across boundaries of estrangement or hostility. The choice is ours. Will the generous texts of our tradition serve as interpretive keys to the rest, or will the abrasive passages determine our ideas of what we are and what we are called on to do? No tradition is free from the constant need to reinterpret, to apply eternal truths to an ever-changing world, to listen to what God's word requires of me, here, now. That is what religious leaders have always done, in the past no less than now.

The question is: To what extent will we see our present interconnectedness as a threat or a challenge? As the work of man, or as a call from God to a greater humanity, as well as to a greater self-restraint? As for me, I believe that we are being summoned by God to see in the human other a trace of the divine Other. The test – so lamentably failed by the great powers of the twentieth century – is to see the divine presence in the face of a stranger; to heed the cry of those who are disempowered in this age of unprecedented powers; who are hungry and poor and ignorant and uneducated, whose human potential is being denied the chance to be expressed. That is the faith of Abraham and Sarah, from whom the great faiths, Judaism, Christianity and Islam, trace their spiritual or actual ancestry. That is the faith of one who, though he called himself but dust and ashes, asked of God himself, 'Shall the judge of all the earth not do justice?' We are not gods, but we are summoned by God – to do His work of love and justice and compassion and peace.

Many years ago I had the privilege of meeting one of the great religious leaders of the Jewish world. He was the head of a large group of Jewish mystics. I was inspired by his teachings and impressed by the spirituality of his followers. But I had a question about the way of life he advocated. It seemed exclusive. In its intense and segregated piety it shut out the rest of the world. Was there not – I asked him – beauty and value outside the narrow walls in which he lived? He answered me with a parable.

Imagine, he said, two people who spend their lives transporting stones. One carries bags of diamonds. The other hauls sacks of rocks. Each is now asked to take a consignment of rubies. Which of the two understands what he is now to carry? The man who is used to diamonds knows that stones can be precious, even those that are not diamonds. But the man who has carried only rocks thinks of stones as a mere burden. They have weight but not worth. Rubies are beyond his comprehension.

So it is, he said, with faith. If we cherish our own, then we will understand the value of others. We may regard ours as a diamond and another faith as a ruby, but we know that both are precious stones. But if faith is a mere burden, not only will we not value ours. Neither will we value the faith of someone else. We will see both as equally useless. True tolerance, he implied, comes not from the absence of faith but from its living presence. Understanding the particularity of what matters to us is the best way of coming to appreciate what matters to others.

Difference does not diminish; it enlarges the sphere of human possibilities. Our last best hope is to recall the classic statement of John Donne and the more ancient story of Noah after the Flood and hear, in the midst of our hypermodernity, an old–new call to a global covenant of human responsibility and hope. Only when we realize the danger of wishing that everyone should be the same – the same faith on the one hand, the same McWorld on the other – will we prevent the clash of civilizations, born of the sense of threat and fear. We will learn to live with diversity once we understand the God-given, world-enhancing dignity of difference.

NOTES

1. Novak 1991.
2. Fukuyama 1992, p. 328.
3. Ibid., p. 330.
4. Ibid., p. 332.
5. Plamenatz 1963, p. 50.
6. Ignatieff 1993, p. 188.
7. Selznick 1994, p. 480.
8. Michael Fishbane, 'Torah and Tradition', in Douglas Knight (ed.), *Tradition and Theology in the Old Testament* (Philadelphia, PA: Fortress Press, 1977), p. 278; see also Michael Fishbane, *Biblical Interpretation in Ancient Israel* (Oxford, Clarendon Press, 1985), pp. 367–8.
9. Burke 1993, p. 96.
10. Selznick 1994, p. 483.

Bibliography

Abrams, Elliott (2001), *The Influence of Faith*. Lanham, MD: Rowman & Littlefield.

Acton, H. B. (1993), *The Morals of Markets and Related Essays*. Indianapolis, IN: Liberty Press.

Adorno, T. W. (1982), *The Authoritarian Personality*. New York: W. W. Norton

Althusius, Johannes (1995), *Politica*. Indianapolis, IN: Liberty Press.

Anderson, Benedict (1991), *Imagined Communities*. London: Verso.

Aristotle (1988), *The Politics* (ed. Stephen Everson). Cambridge: Cambridge University Press.

Barber, Benjamin (1992), 'Jihad vs. McWorld', *Atlantic Monthly* (March).

—— (2001), *Jihad vs McWorld*. New York: Ballantine.

Baron, Salo (1945), *The Jewish Community*, Vol. 2. Philadelphia, PA: Jewish Publication Society.

Barzun, Jacques (2000), *From Dawn to Decadence*. New York: HarperCollins.

Baum, Gregory and Wells, Harold (eds) (1997), *The Reconciliation of Peoples*. New York: Orbis.

Bauman, Zygmunt (1998), *Globalization: The Human Consequences*. Cambridge: Polity Press.

Bellah, Robert, Madsen, Richard, Sullivan, William, Swidler, Ann and Tipton, Steven (1988), *Habits of the Heart*. London: Hutchinson.

Bentley, Tom and Stedman Jones, Daniel (2001), *The Moral Universe*. London: Demos.

Berger, Peter (1967), *The Sacred Canopy*, New York: Doubleday.

—— (ed.) (1999), *The Desecularization of the World*. Grand Rapids, MI: Eerdmans.

—— Berger, Brigitte and Kellner, Hansfried (1973), *The Homeless Mind*. London: Penguin.

Berlin, Isaiah (2002), *Liberty*. Oxford: Oxford University Press.

Booth, Ken, Dunne, Tim and Cox, Michael (eds) (2001), *How Might we Live? Global Ethics in the New Century*. Cambridge: Cambridge University Press.

Brown, Gordon (2002), *Tackling Poverty: A Global New Deal*. London: HM Treasury.

Brown, William P. (1999), *The Ethos of the Cosmos*. Grand Rapids, MI: Eerdmans.

Brittan, Samuel (1995), *Capitalism with a Human Face*. London: Edward Elgar.

Buber, Martin (1996), *Paths in Utopia*. Syracuse, NY: Syracuse University Press.

Burke, Edmund (1993), *Reflections on the Revolution in France*. Oxford: Oxford University Press.

Burley, Justine (1999), *The Genetic Revolution and Human Rights*. Oxford: Oxford University Press.

Cahill, Thomas (1999), *The Gifts of the Jews*. New York: Anchor.

Clinton, Bill (2001), 'The Struggle for the Soul of the 21st Century', BBC, Dimbleby Lecture (14 December).

Cupitt, Don (1984), *The Sea of Faith*. London: BBC.

Dale, Graham (2000), *God's Politicians*. London: HarperCollins.

Demos (1998), *The Good Life*. London: Demos.

Dennis, Norman and Halsey, A. H. (1988), *English Ethical Socialism*. Oxford: Clarendon Press.

Diamond, Jared (1992), *The Third Chimpanzee*. New York: Harper Perennial.

Dionne, E. J. (1998), *Community Works*. Washington, DC: Brookings Institution.

Diringer, David (1958), *The Story of the Aleph Beth*. London: Lincolns-Prager.

—— (1962), *Writing*. London: Thames & Hudson.

Donne, John (1930), *Complete Poetry and Selected Prose*. London: Nonesuch.

Dunning, J. H. (1997), *Alliance Capitalism and Global Business*. London and New York: Routledge.

—— (2002), 'Relational Capital, Networks and International Business Activity', in F. Contractor and P. Lorange, *Cooperative Strategies and Alliances*. Oxford: Elsevier Science (forthcoming).

Eberly, Don (ed.) (1994), *Building a Community of Citizens*. Lanham, MD:

University Press of America.

—— (ed.) (2000), *The Essential Civil Society Reader*. Lanham, MD: Rowman & Littlefield.

Elazar, Daniel (1989), *People and Polity*. Detroit, MI: Wayne State University Press.

—— (1995), *Covenant and Polity in Biblical Israel*. New Brunswick: Transaction.

—— (1998), *Covenant and Civil Society*. New Brunswick: Transaction.

Enright, Robert and North, Joanna (eds) (1998), *Exploring Forgiveness*. Madison, WI: University of Wisconsin Press.

Etzioni, Amitai and Carney, David (eds), (1997), *Repentance: A Comparative Perspective*. Lanham, MD: Rowman & Littlefield.

Finkielkraut, Alain (2001), *In the Name of Humanity*. London: Pimlico.

Frank, Thomas (2002), *One Market Under God*. London: Vintage.

Friedman, Thomas (2000), *The Lexus and the Olive Tree*. London: HarperCollins.

Fukuyama, Francis (1989), 'The End of History?', *The National Interest*, 16 (Summer): 3-18.

—— (1992), *The End of History and the Last Man*. London: Hamish Hamilton.

—— (1995), *Trust*. London: Hamish Hamilton.

—— (1999), *The Great Disruption*. London: Profile.

Galbraith, John Kenneth (1992), *The Culture of Contentment*. London: Sinclair-Stevenson.

George, Henry (1907), *Moses*, Lecture given in St Andrew's Hall, Glasgow, 28 December 1884. Glasgow: Land Values Publication Dept.

Gladwell, Malcolm (2001), *The Tipping Point*. London: Abacus.

Glendon, M. and Blankenhorn, D. (eds) (1995), *Seedbeds of Virtue*. Lanham, MD: Madison Books.

Glover, Jonathan (1999), *Humanity*. London: Jonathan Cape.

Gompertz, Lewis (1992), *Moral Inquiries on the Situation of Man and the Beasts*, Fontwell, Sussex: Centaur Press.

Gopin, Marc (2000), *Between Eden and Armageddon*. Oxford: Oxford University Press.

Gottwald, Norman K. (1980), *The Tribes of Yahweh*. London: SCM Press.

Gray, John (1997), *Endgames*. Oxford: Blackwell.

Gunton, Colin (1993), *The One, The Three and The Many*. Cambridge: Cambridge University Press.

Harrison, Lawrence and Huntington, Samuel (eds) (2000), *Culture Matters*. New York: Basic Books.

Havel, Václav (1998), *The Art of the Impossible*. New York: Fromm.

Held, David (ed.) (2000), *A Globalizing World?* London: Routledge.

Held, David and McGrew, Anthony (eds) (2000), *The Global Transformations Reader*. Cambridge: Polity Press.

Henderson, Michael (2002), *Forgiveness: Breaking the Chain of Hate*. London: Grosvenor Books.

Hertz, Noreena (2001), *The Silent Takeover*. London: William Heinemann.

Heschel, A. J. (1962), *The Prophets*. Philadelphia, PA: Jewish Publication Society.

Hill, Christopher (1994), *The English Bible and the Seventeenth Century Revolution*. London: Penguin.

Hillers, Delbert (1969), *Covenant: The History of a Biblical Idea*. Baltimore, MD: Johns Hopkins University Press.

Hirsch, Samson Raphael (1969), *The Nineteen Letters*. New York: Feldheim.

Hirschman, Albert (1997), *The Passions and the Interests*. Princeton, NJ: Princeton University Press.

Hobbes, Thomas (1991), *Leviathan*. Cambridge: Cambridge University Press.

Howard, Michael (2000), *The Invention of Peace*. London: Profile.

Huntington, Samuel (1996), *The Clash of Civilizations and the Remaking of World Order*. New York: Simon & Schuster.

Ignatieff, Michael (1993), *Blood and Belonging*. London: Viking.

—— (1997), *The Warrior's Honor*. New York: Metropolitan Books.

—— (2001), *Human Rights as Politics and Idolatry*. Princeton, NJ: Princeton University Press.

James, Oliver (1997), *Britain on the Couch*. London: Century.

Jay, Peter (2001), *Road to Riches*. London: Phoenix.

Johnston, Douglas and Sampson, Cynthia (eds) (1994), *Religion, The Missing Dimension of Statecraft*. Oxford: Oxford University Press.

Jonas, Hans (1984), *The Imperative of Responsibility*. Chicago, IL: University of Chicago Press.

—— (1996), *Mortality and Morality*. Evanston, IL: Northwestern University Press.

Klein, Naomi (2001), *No Logo*. London: Flamingo.

Korten, David (2000), *Post-Corporate world*. West Hartford, CT: Kumarian.

Landes, David (1998), *The Wealth and Poverty of Nations*. London: Little, Brown & Co.

Lang, Berel (1996), *Heidegger's Silence*. London: Athlone Press.

Lasch, Christopher, (1991), *The True and Only Heaven*. New York: W. W. Norton.

Leadbeater, Charles (2000), *Living on Thin Air*. London: Penguin.

Levi, Primo (1987), *If This is a Man*. London: Abacus.

Lindblom, Johannes (1962), *Prophecy in Ancient Israel*. Oxford: Blackwell.

MacIntyre, Alasdair (1981), *After Virtue*. London: Duckworth.

Man, John (2001), *Alpha Beta: How our Alphabet Shaped the Western World*. London: Headline.

Meilaender, Gilbert (2000), *Working: Its Meaning and Its Limits*. Notre Dame, IN: University of Notre Dame Press.

Mendes-Flohr, Paul and Reinharz, Judah (1980), *The Jew in the Modern World*. New York: Oxford.

Micklethwait, John and Woolridge, Adrian (2001), *A Future Perfect*. London: Random House.

Monbiot, George (2001), *Captive State: The Corporate Takeover of Britain*. London: Pan.

Moore, K. and Lewis, D. (1999), *Birth of the Multinational*. Copenhagen: Copenhagen Business Press.

Naisbitt, John and Aburdene, Patricia (1990), *Megatrends 2000*. London: Sidgwick & Jackson.

Nisbet, Robert (1980), *History of the Idea of Progress*. New York: Basic Books.

Novak, Michael (1991), *The Spirit of Democratic Capitalism*. London: Institute of Economic Affairs.

—— (1992), *This Hemisphere of Liberty*. Washington, DC: American Enterprise Institute.

—— (1993), *The Catholic Ethic and the Spirit of Capitalism*. New York: Free Press.

—— (1996) *Business as a Calling*. New York: Free Press.

—— (1999), *On Cultivating Liberty*. Lanham, MD: Rowman & Littlefield.

Nye, Joseph S. (2002), *The Paradox of American Power*. New York: Oxford University Press.

Ogburn, William (1964), *Social Change*. Gloucester, MA: Peter Smith.

Ong, Walter J. (1992), *Orality and Literacy*. London: Routledge.

Passmore, John (1980), *Man's Responsibility for Nature*. London: Duckworth.

Perlas, Nicanor (2000), *Shaping Globalization*. Philippines: Centre for Alternative Development Initiatives.

Picco, Giandomenico (2001), *Crossing the Divide: Dialogue Among Civilizations*. South Orange, NJ: Seton Hall University.

Plamenatz, John (1963), *Man and Society*, Vol. 1. London: Longman.

Plato (1955), *The Republic* (trans. H. D. P. Lee). Harmondsworth: Penguin.

Rawls, John (1993), *Political Liberalism*. New York: Columbia University Press.

—— (1999), *The Law of Peoples*. Cambridge, MA: Harvard University Press.

Reich, Robert (1992), *The Work of Nations*, New York: Vintage.

—— (2001), *The Future of Success*. London: William Heinemann.

Ridley, Matt (1996), *The Origins of Virtue*. London: Viking.

—— (1999), *Genome*. London: Fourth Estate.

Rifkin, Jeremy (1999), *The Biotech Century*. London: Phoenix.

—— (2000), *The Age of Access*. London: Penguin.

Rorty, Richard (1980), *Philosophy and the Mirror of Nature*. Oxford: Blackwell.

—— (1989), *Contingency, Irony and Solidarity*. Cambridge: Cambridge University Press.

Rotenstreich, Nathan (1984), *Jews and German Philosophy*. New York: Schocken.

Sacks, Jonathan (1990), *Tradition in an Untraditional Age*. London: Vallentine Mitchell.

—— (1995), *Community of Faith*. London: Peter Halban.

—— (1999) *Morals and Markets*. London: Institute of Economic Affairs.

—— (2000), *The Politics of Hope*, 2nd edn. London: Vintage.

—— (2001), *Radical Then, Radical Now*. London: HarperCollins.

Sandel, Michael (1982), *Liberalism and the Limits of Justice*. Cambridge: Cambridge University Press.

—— (ed.) (1984), *Liberalism and its Critics*. Oxford: Blackwell.

Schumpeter, Joseph (1947), *Capitalism, Socialism and Democracy*. London: George Allen & Unwin.

Scruton, Roger (1996), *Animal Rights and Wrongs*. London: Demos.

—— (1998), *An Intelligent Person's Guide to Modern Culture*. London: Duckworth.

Seligman, Adam (1997), *The Problem of Trust*. Princeton, NJ: Princeton University Press.

Selznick, Philip (1994), *The Moral Commonwealth*. Berkeley, CA: University of California Press.

Sen, Amartya (1999), *Development as Freedom*. Oxford: Oxford University Press.

Shriver, Donald (1995), *An Ethic for Enemies*. Oxford: Oxford University Press.

Smith, Adam (1937), *An Inquiry into the Nature and Causes of the Wealth of Nations*. New York: Modern Library.

—— (1976), *The Theory of Moral Sentiments*. Indianapolis, IN: Liberty Press.

—— (1986), *The Wealth of Nations, Books I–III*. London: Penguin Classics.

Sombart, Werner (1997), *The Jews and Modern Capitalism*. New Brunswick: Transaction.

Soros, George (1998), *The Crisis of Global Capitalism*. London: Little, Brown & Co.

—— (2000), *Open Society: Reforming Global Capitalism*. London: Little, Brown & Co.

—— (2002), *On Globalization*. Oxford: Public Affairs.

Stackhouse, Max (ed.) (2000), *God and Globalization. Volume 1: Religion and the Powers of the Common Life*. Harrisburg, PA: Trinity Press International.

—— (2001), *God and Globalization, Volume 2: The Spirit and the Modern Authorities*. Harrisburg, PA: Trinity Press International.

Stitskin, Leon (1982), *Letters of Maimonides*. New York: Yeshiva University Press.

Tabb, William (2001), *The Amoral Elephant*. New York: Monthly Review Press.

—— (2002), *Unequal Partners*. New York: New Press.

Tamari, Meir (1987), *With All Your Possessions: Jewish Ethics and Economic Life*. New York: Free Press.

—— (1995), *The Challenge of Wealth*. Northvale, NJ: Jason Aronson.

Tocqueville, Alexis de (1968), *Democracy in America*. London: Fontana.

Toffler, Alvin (1971), *Future Shock*. London: Pan.

Voegelin, Eric (1956), *Order and History. Volume 1, Israel and Revelation*. Columbia, MO: University of Missouri Press.

Walzer, Michael (1994), *Thick and Thin*. Notre Dame, IN: University of Notre Dame Press.

—— (ed.) (1995), *Toward a Global Civil Society*. Providence, RI: Berghahn Books.

Warren, Mark (ed.) (1999), *Democracy and Trust*. Cambridge: Cambridge University Press.

—— (2001), *Democracy and Association*. Princeton, NJ: Princeton University Press.

Weber, Max (1952), *Ancient Judaism*. New York: Free Press.

—— (1985), *The Protestant Ethic and the Spirit of Capitalism*. London: Unwin.

Wells, H. G. (n.d.), *The Study of History*. London: George Newnes.

Whitehead, Alfred North (1942), *Adventures of Ideas*. Harmondsworth: Penguin.

Williams, Bernard (1985), *Ethics and the Limits of Philosophy*. London: Fontana.

Wilson, Edward O. (1999), *Consilience*. London: Abacus.

Wright, Robert (1995), *The Moral Animal*. London: Little, Brown & Co.

—— (2000), *Nonzero: The Logic of Human Destiny*. New York: Pantheon.